T0317652

TRADING THE
MEASURED MOVE

TRADING THE MEASURED MOVE

A Path to Trading Success
in a World of Algos and
High-Frequency Trading

David M. Halsey

WILEY

Published by John Wiley & Sons, Inc., Hoboken, New Jersey.
Published simultaneously in Canada.

Limit of Liability/Disclaimer of Warranty: While the publisher and author have used their best efforts
in preparing this book, they make no representations or warranties with respect to the accuracy
or completeness of the contents of this book and specifically disclaim any implied warranties of
merchantability or fitness for a particular purpose. No warranty may be created or extended by
sales representatives or written sales materials. The advice and strategies contained herein may not
be suitable for your situation. You should consult with a professional where appropriate. Neither the
publisher nor author shall be liable for any loss of profit or any other commercial damages, including
but not limited to special, incidental, consequential, or other damages.

For general information on our other products and services or for technical support, please contact
our Customer Care Department within the United States at (800) 762-2974, outside the United
States at (317) 572-3993, or fax (317) 572-4002.

Wiley publishes in a variety of print and electronic formats and by print-on-demand. Some material
included with standard print versions of this book may not be included in e-books or in print-
on-demand. If this book refers to media such as a CD or DVD that is not included in the version
you purchased, you may download this material at http://booksupport.wiley.com. For more
information about Wiley products, visit www.wiley.com.

Library of Congress Cataloging-in-Publication Data:
Halsey, David M., 1977-
    Trading the measured move : a path to trading success in a world of algos and high frequency
trading / David M. Halsey.
        pages cm. — (Wiley trading series)
    Includes index.
    ISBN 978-1-118-25183-6 (cloth); ISBN 978-1-118-28713-2 (ePDF);
    ISBN 978-1-118-28332-5 (ePub)
    1. Investment analysis.   2. Algorithms.   3. Program trading (Securities)
    4. Electronic trading of securities.   I. Title.
    HG4529.H356 2014
    332.64'20285—dc23
                                                                                    2013029212

Printed in the United States of America.
10 9 8 7 6 5 4 3 2 1

I would like to dedicate this book to my dad, who taught me that excellence is a habit and that there is no such thing as luck. What others mistake as luck is where preparation meets opportunity.

CONTENTS

CONTENTS

In today's financial markets, each time a retail trader places a stock, options, or futures trade, he or she enters a world dominated by massive amounts of capital allocated by algorithms designed by brilliant mathematical minds and running on the ultra-fast computers of the world's largest financial institutions. Through years of research and trading experience I have discovered a means by which an individual retail trader can face that daunting competition and win. This book provides you with both the broad background and the necessary details of how to trade courageously and profitably in today's markets.

■ Who This Book Is For and Why It's Important

Traders at all levels of experience will benefit from reading this book. Advanced traders will be familiar with most of the book's terminology but most likely will not be familiar with its new and unique approach to the use of Fibonacci retracements within a series of measured moves or with the structure of nested measured moves across multiple time frames. For beginning traders, a glossary provides definitions and basic information regarding all technical terms used in the book. Armed with this information, beginners will be able to understand and implement the methodology detailed in the book's body. Intermediate traders who might have floundered in today's market while testing indicator after indicator and method after method will find relief in this book's clear, precise, and proven methodology. All traders will benefit from sidebars that tell stories of my personal experiences that lead to specific discoveries and aha moments in the development of this methodology.

Algorithmic trading strategies based on sophisticated quantitative analysis and often employing high frequency trading (HFT) tactics have in recent years given enormous market advantages to the largest financial institutions in the world. Put simply, in the world of trading and investing, the quants, as they are known, have changed the rules for the foreseeable future and have placed the individual retail trader at an unprecedented disadvantage—that is, unless that trader learns a new way of trading that strives to ride the waves created by the quants' trading activity with confidence and to capture consistent profits along the way. This book offers the individual trader a blueprint for creating such a trading plan built on a dynamic framework of fundamental principles flexible enough to support his or her own trading personality.

■ Fibs Make the Moves

Through years of exhaustive research combined with trial-and-error trading on the playing field of futures, options, and equities, I have identified an undiscovered set of trading rules commonly used by the quants. Armed with this knowledge, I developed a unique and powerful methodology for successfully navigating this new and previously uncharted trading environment. At the core of this methodology is the measured move, as described by Fibonnaci retracements. Put simply, Fibs make the moves. The reason that this is so is that the trading activity of the quants makes it so. The methodology here offers a means for the retail trader to ride the coattails of massive amounts of institutional money and to make substantial profits along the way.

My trading methodology surrounds the concept of Fibonnaci-based measured moves with a kit of tools specialized for each trading instrument. Through my research I have unveiled the personalities of a wide range of trading instruments, each created by the movement of substantial amounts of institutional capital each trading day. In order for a retail trader to profit from riding the coattails of this capital, the trader must know which market internals the institutional algorithms are tracking. For example, when trading the ES futures contract based on the Standard & Poor's (S&P) 500 stock index, the quants habitually buy or sell based not on Fibonnaci levels alone but also based on New York Stock Exchange (NYSE) tick, particularly at the extremities of its range. The Bank index, which tracks the Nasdaq's largest financial components, is critically useful as a gauge of overall market sentiment. Finally, the use of tick charts (not to be confused with NYSE tick) and the fine art of tape reading allow a trader to make accurate judgments on price movement for specific instruments based on institutional participation or lack thereof.

This book makes the case that in today's new trading environment of institutional algorithms and high-frequency trading the traditional lagging indicators such as moving average convergence/divergence (MACD) and stochastics used by most retail traders do not work. The quants don't use them, so retail traders shouldn't use them either. Instead, retail traders who read this book should learn to use what the quants use—Fibonnaci-based measured moves and market internals specific to each trading instrument. Armed with a solid understanding of each along with a fully prepared, attentive, and realistic psychological inner state, the retail trader can enter today's trading environment as a successful and profitable participant.

ACKNOWLEDGMENTS

I would like to thank my wife for helping me along the way in the writing of this book. Without her, it would not have been possible. I would also like to thank my editor Jennifer MacDonald for putting up with me during the editing process and her amazing patience. Without her accountability and motivation, the book would not be possible.

CHAPTER 1

Today's Trading Environment

Descent of the Pit and Ascent of the Screen

In the opening moments of *Floored*, James Allen Smith's incisive documentary about the decline of Chicago's trading pits, two telling statistics flash across the screen:

- In 1997, more than 10,000 traders traded on pit floors.

- In 2009, approximately 1,000 pit traders remained.

What happened? In a word, computers. In a phrase, computers replaced people. Actually, it's not quite that simple. Like most sea changes in human activities, the change from *open outcry* trading to a fully electronic, often automated, trading environment has been a gradual one. What was once a cacophonous scene of sweaty humans bellowing buy and sell orders while avoiding the elbows of other traders packed into the pit like sardines in a can has been transformed into a market dominated by the cleanly efficient hum of rack upon rack of digital servers placing millions of orders per second. Since Nasdaq emerged in 1971 as the world's first electronic stock market, the use of computers in trading has marched forward with the crushing momentum of an advancing army passing milestone after milestone:

- 1992: The Chicago Mercantile Exchange (CME), founded in 1898, opened Globex, a 24-hour market for trading futures.

- 1997: The London Stock Exchange (LSE), founded in 1801, opened an electronic trading market. The same year, the Toronto Stock Exchange (then TSE, now TSX), founded in 1861, did the same.

- 2000: New York's International Securities Exchange (ISE) opened the first electronic options exchange.

- 2003–2004: Chicago's Citadel Investment Group unleashed its high-frequency trading (HFT) system for U.S. equity options.

- 2006: The venerable New York Stock Exchange (NYSE), founded in 1863, merged with Archipelago Exchange (ArcaEx), an electronic communications network (ECN) founded in 1997.

Along the way, there were many other milestones—too many to list here—but the implications of this evolution is clear: in the world of *institutional trading,* computers are here to stay, and the open outcry trading pit is nearing its last days.

The implications for you, the trader, are not merely academic. In order to trade today's markets successfully and profitably, a trader must know the lay of the land in order to avoid crevasses, drop-offs, patches of quicksand, and myriad other hazards that come with the terrain. Knowing every detail of every hazard is impossible, but knowing what to look out for is invaluable.

■ Players on the Field

So if the vast majority of trading is done outside of the traditional trading pits, where is it being done and by whom? The answers to these questions are, on the one hand, quite clear and simple, and on the other, very murky and complex. What is clearly undeniable is that most trading around the world today is being done electronically—a buyer submits a buy order that is transmitted to a location where it is matched with a sell order submitted by a seller; a trade then executes. That much is simple. Parsing the terms in that simple statement is where murkiness and complexity lie in wait. The first question is: who are the buyers and sellers? Here are several candidates: banks (commercial, retail, investment, private, and central), insurance companies, pension funds, hedge funds, mutual funds, private equity firms, venture capital firms, brokerage houses, algorithmic trading firms, high-frequency trading firms, sovereign wealth funds, municipalities, government agencies, and, finally, *retail traders* like you. All of these players have their own agendas, their own profit motives, and their own sets of strategies and tactics. Some of them trade in multiple markets simultaneously, while others specialize in just one market or a very limited selection of markets. Many of them host rooms full of human traders sitting at multiscreen computers placing trades with mouse clicks. Some, but not many (yet), make exclusive use of program trading *algorithms* that place trades with no human intervention whatsoever. While it's not necessary for a retail trader to know precisely who (or what) is on the other side of a trade, being aware of the players on the field (and their *size*) is essential.

Why is size so important? Because large orders move the market. Large buy orders, especially a series of large buy orders, almost invariably cause price to rise. Conversely, large sell orders, especially in a series, cause price to fall. Econ 101 teaches that supply and demand rule in markets of all types. Increasing demand leads to decreasing supply and rising prices, whereas decreasing demand leads to increasing supply and falling prices. It's true for guns and butter, and it's true for every type of trading instrument—stocks, bonds, futures, options, currencies, commodities, you name it. In Chapter 4, we'll see how tape-reading techniques can help the individual trader gauge the presence or absence of large orders. Being aware of this presence or absence can give a trader an edge—an advantage that can be used in placing profitable trades.

The second question raised above is where do trades take place? In the old days of floor trading in cities like New York, Chicago, Philadelphia, San Francisco, and Minneapolis, the answer was simple. Trades occurred on the floor of the exchanges on which buy and sell orders were placed. A person could see with the naked eye where each trade took place. Today, while a small percentage of trades still occur on the few trading floors that remain, the answer is not quite so simple. While most trades still occur at an exchange, each trade is actually made by software known as a *matching engine,* which runs on a digital server hosted by that exchange. Matching engines do just what their name suggests—they match buy orders with sell orders prior to trade execution. Most matching engines for exchanges based on the East Coast are in New Jersey in places like Weehawken, Secaucus, or Mahwah. Chicago-based exchanges keep their servers in their own sweet home Chicago. Beyond the usual stock, options, and futures exchanges are the infamous and shadowy dark pools, which are private exchanges accessible only to investors capable of placing extremely large orders. Dark pools provide markets in which a huge stock order can be traded anonymously and hidden from public view until the trade has already executed. By hiding large trades from the public eye, traders can avoid price moving against their trades. On a public exchange, a trader's desire to buy or sell a large quantity of stock would be visible to anyone in the market, thereby skewing the current state of supply and demand and potentially moving price away from the trader's target. Dark pools are the subject of much controversy today, with some strongly opposed to their very existence and others highly supportive. Heated debate about their regulation or outright banishment will likely be part of the political landscape for the foreseeable future. For retail traders, however, simply being aware of their existence is sufficient.

■ The Algo Brothers

It was inevitable. The increasing use of digital technology—mainframe computers, personal computers (PCs), server farms, wide-area networks (WANs), local-area networks (LANs), broadband connectivity, and so on— would one day give rise to the birth of the algorithmic trade. Anyone opening an account today with any online brokerage will have nearly instantaneous access to mountain upon mountain of market data, much of it delivered in real time and often for free. Even neophytes today have access to a real-time data feed that wouldn't have entered the wildest dreams of legendary early Wall Street traders such as Jesse Livermore or Richard Wyckoff. Sophisticated charting programs allow traders to customize the way in which these mountains of data are presented graphically. Indeed, a picture is often worth a thousand words (or columns of numbers). The ubiquity and ease of data access is so pervasive today that it's easy to take it for granted. Be that as it may, rest assured that if even a beginning retail trader has access to volumes of market data, the large trading firms have it as well and in spades. And what they do with those data goes way beyond painting a pretty picture with it.

In today's financial markets, each time you place a stock, options, or futures trade, you enter a world dominated by massive amounts of capital allocated by algorithms designed by brilliant mathematical minds and running on the ultra-fast computers of the world's largest financial institutions. Over the past decade, firms like Goldman Sachs, UBS, Barclay's, Morgan Stanley, and many others put two and two together and saw the gold in them thar hills of data laid out before them. After first recognizing the tremendous untapped profit potential buried in these data, they set their sights on mining them. Being of extremely deep pockets, they created rooms full of PhDs packing formidable knowledge in mathematics and computer science. From this knowledge and countless man-hours of algorithm design and computer coding came programs capable of mining torrents of data, extracting salient bits of market information, and placing trades based on that information. This kind of program trading based not on *fundamentals* but instead on *quantitative analysis* of *technical data* is called quant trading; its practitioners are known simply as *quants.* No one knows exactly how pervasive quant trading is in today's markets; the estimates range from 60 percent to 80 percent of daily market volume or more. Suffice it to say that quant trading is a major part of today's market structure. In fact, many market observers believe a major cause of the Flash Crash of May 6, 2010, was that the vast majority of algorithmic trading programs backed away en masse from the *bid-ask spread,* resulting in a lack of demand and a concomitant and extraordinarily rapid drop in price.

The Flash Crash proved the adage that, indeed, when there's nobody willing to buy, price will inevitably and inexorably fall. The harrowing episode in market history that was the Flash Crash begs the question: when program trading has the potential to cause such severe market disruption, why would anyone choose to practice it? An answer can be found in extensive media coverage from 2009, when it was reported that Goldman Sachs had achieved record quarterly profits, much of it attributable to its program trading. As is usually the case, if the profit potential is there, they will come. Increasingly, most institutional traders practice at least some program trading, and some do nothing but. More and more, trading desks are being replaced by trading racks. May the best algo win.

In reality, this process of market data extraction and trade decision making based on information gleaned from those data is nothing new. That's what Jesse Livermore did at the turn of the twentieth century, too. But he did it based on numbers on a chalkboard or on paper tape spit out by a clacking ticker-tape machine. The differences today—and they are *huge*—are of volume and speed. In days of old, trading occurred at the speed of word-of-mouth. Today, trades move with the speed of electron motion. And that brings us to the latest form of program trading, one that can be seen as the hyperactive brother within the Algo family: high-frequency trading (HFT). Just as the advent of program trading in the global marketplace was an inevitable consequence of the introduction of electronic trading, so is HFT. But just as traditional program trading uses many techniques of quantitative analysis that have been around for years, so does HFT make use of some not-so-new techniques—those of the scalpers. For years, successful scalpers have combined eagle-eyed chart-reading skills with quick reflexes and trigger fingers worthy of the best video gamers to rack up similarly quick profits from trades lasting just seconds. Scalpers jump into a moving stream of price and jump out almost immediately, taking their catch with them. Well, actually, *immediately* is used here in a relative sense. What might seem immediate when measured on a human scale would be considered absolutely slothlike from the perspective of an HFT trading platform.

So, what do HFT traders do and who are they? In the most general sense, HFT platforms use extremely fast computers to place extremely quick trades based on profit opportunities discovered by their algorithms. Think scalpers on steroids. Whereas a human scalper might have a couple or even several screens of charts and rapidly moving columns of price and volume data flashing before his or her eyes, many HFT platforms have the whole world of market data flowing into their buffers every second of every day. Think of it: *all* of the options, futures, bonds, currency, and equity data from *all* of the world's markets at *all* times of day and night just waiting to be parsed and analyzed by blindingly fast banks of computers. But all of that data wealth would be wasted if not for very, very smart software trained to see profit opportunity and to act on it. For that reason, most HFT firms follow the traditional program trading model of employing the best and brightest mathematicians and computer scientists for their programming teams. As a group, HFT firms tend to be a quiet bunch. Until very recently, they preferred to operate out of the public eye, almost as if in the shadows. The Flash Crash changed all of that. In the aftermath of that remarkable market disruption, HFT was often singled out by market watchdogs as one of the likely culprits at fault. As a result, 31 of the largest HFT firms have banded together into the Principal Traders Group, presumably in part to tell their side of the story in their own defense. You really can't blame them for banding together; the head of the Securities and Exchange Commission (SEC) has called for a thorough examination of the role of HFT in the Flash Crash and the commissioner of the Commodity Futures Trading Commission (CFTC) has characterized HFT traders as cheetahs first to the kill in the markets. The bottom line: increased regulation of HFT in the near future is highly likely.

While an exhaustive investigation of HFT goes beyond the scope of this book, a few of its strategies and tactics are worth mentioning, if nothing else because they have such colorful names. In his book *All About High-Frequency Trading* (McGraw-Hill, 2010), HFT pioneer Michael Durbin lists the following HFT techniques: Penny Jump, Push the Elephant, Tow the Iceberg, Jump the Delta, Rebate Scratching, and Slow-Mover Takeout, among others. While each has its own set of unique characteristics, many of them seek to capitalize on market imbalances through *arbitrage* of one sort or another.

For example, if one HFT platform sees that it can buy a *trading instrument* in one market at a lower price and sell it in another at a higher price, it will attempt to capitalize on that opportunity instantaneously before another HFT platform is able to do so. Speed is of the absolute essence; a delay of even a few milliseconds in either trade entry or exit will often make the difference between a winning trade and a losing trade. For this reason, and understandably so, many HFT firms colocate their servers in the same buildings as the servers run by the major exchanges. Therefore, there are many HFT servers in New Jersey and Chicago. When milliseconds matter, you want your trade submissions to travel the shortest distance possible.

■ Where Are You?

After reading the last few pages profiling the gigantic financial and trading resources unleashed by the biggest players in the market every day, you, as an individual retail trader, might be feeling pretty small right now. You might see yourself as a very small David against a very large Goliath. But wait, who won that battle? David did.

The goal of this book is to demonstrate that a retail trader armed with a sound trading plan based on proven technical analysis along with a strong commitment to trading discipline can succeed and profit consistently in a marketplace dominated by giants. Bringing down Goliath with a single shot? Certainly not. But trading profitably on a consistent basis day after day, week after week, year after year? Absolutely.

Every successful campaign, whether in war, sports, politics, marketing, or whatever, contains two primary elements: strategy and tactics. It is very important to understand the difference between the two. A campaign's strategy is an overall plan designed to achieve the campaign's goal. Tactics are a set of individual, particular techniques applied step by step in order to complete a given strategy. For a retail trader the goal is consistent profitability. The strategy presented in this book for achieving that goal is to follow the money, to ride the coattails of the Big Players, to play the game just as Smart Money does. A discussion of our tactics follows in the remainder of this book.

CHAPTER 2

Inside the Hidden Market

A nyone who has ever looked at a stock chart knows that price moves up and price moves down as time marches on. This truism operates on all time frames from those calibrated with miniscule time increments—30-second, 1-minute, 2-minute, and so on—to those with very large time increments—1-week, 1-month, or even 1-year. Price moves up, price moves down, this much is always true. Still, questions remain: *How* does price move in one direction or the other? Are there patterns behind price movement? If there are patterns, can they be perceived by an individual trader? And if so, are these perceived patterns reliable?

■ Deep Roots

These questions and more have been thoroughly investigated by countless market observers, commentators, and traders at least since Munehisa Homma devised a method of trading in the rice markets of eighteenth-century Japan that over time evolved into what is known today as candlestick trading. Homma's method is not the only one with ancient roots, however. Enter Mr. Fibonacci.

Leonardo Pisano Bigollo was a brilliant mathematician who lived in thirteenth-century Italy. Like many of his time, he was known by several different names, the most famous of which is Fibonacci (fih-buh-NAH-chee). During his lifetime he was widely known through his *Book of Calculation,* in which he advocated the use of Arabic numbers (0–9), a radical notion for the Europe of that time. In addition, he discussed the series of numbers we now call the Fibonacci series. Although he didn't invent this series, in his book he applied it to a mathematical problem far removed from the world of trading—the growth of a population of rabbits. Before we move from rabbits to trading, consider these two characteristics of the Fibonacci series:

- Each number is the sum of the two preceding numbers: 0, 1, 1, 2, 3, 5, 8, 13, 21, 34, 55, 89, 144, 233, 377 ...

- Dividing a number in the series by its neighbor to the left results in a number close to 1.618. Numbers further to the right in the series generate results closer to 1.618 than numbers toward the beginning of the series. (Try this with a calculator—it works).

The number 1.618 has long held special significance in the realms of mathematics and the arts, as well as being inherent in many structures in the natural world. It is known as the Golden Ratio and has been a subject of fascination and inquiry for at least 2,400 years since Euclid first defined it in his book *Elements.* It results when a line is divided into two segments, *a* and *b,* so that the relationship between the entire line (*a* + *b*) to the longer segment (*a*) is identical to the relationship between the longer segment (*a*) to the shorter one (*b*) (see Figure 2.1). When these conditions are met, the ratio is deemed golden. To see how this works with the Fibonacci series, take these three adjacent numbers: 89, 144, 233. Call 144 *a* and 89 *b.* Using Figure 2.1 as a guide, add *a* to *b*: 89 + 144 = 233. Divide *a* by *b*: 144 / 89 = 1.6179775 (close enough to 1.618). Next, divide *a* + *b* by *a*: 233 / 144 = 1.6180555 (also close to 1.618).

As so often happens when applying mathematics to both natural and man-made objects, the relationship between the Fibonacci series and the Golden Ratio is not precise down to the last decimal point. But it's been close enough to attract the attention of brilliant minds for much of recorded history. The seventeenth-century German mathematician and astronomer Johannes Kepler called the Golden Ratio a "precious jewel" and combined it with the Pythagorean Theorem in a formulation known as the Kepler Triangle. Artists from Leonardo da Vinci to Salvador Dali have made use of it in their art. Composers such as Bartok and Debussy have used it as a structural element in their music. But it is perhaps within the realm of nature that the presence of the Golden Ratio is the most remarkable. For over 150 years scientists have known that branching patterns of plants and the arrangement of veins in leaves follow the Golden Ratio. So do the structures of pinecones, the

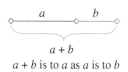

FIGURE 2.1   The Golden Ratio

spiral curvatures found in many sea shells, and the growth patterns of seeds in plants such as the sunflower.[1] The study of the Golden Ratio didn't stop when we rolled into the current millennium. Over the past decade, neurobiologists have identified relationships between the Golden Ratio and the clock cycle of brain waves. In the world of nano-scale quantum mechanics, the Golden Ratio has been found in the magnetic resonance of certain crystals.

Beyond 1.618

Later in the book, we will see that 1.618 carries considerable significance when applied to price movement in the world of trading. Before getting to that, here are a few more Fibonacci facts:

- Dividing a number in the series by its neighbor to the right results in a number close to .618. Hmm, where have we seen that sequence of numbers before?

- Dividing a number in the series by its neighbor two to the right results in a number close to .382.

- Dividing a number in the series by its neighbor three to the right results in a number close to .236.

Two of these three numbers—.618 and .236—along with one non-Fibonacci number long familiar to almost everyone—.50—form the heart of the Fibonacci-based trading methodology presented in this book. By the time you've finish reading, you'll know them like the back of your hand.

■ Fibonacci Basics

Many technical traders have a seemingly insatiable appetite for more and more indicators as if there could never be enough of them. For example, one popular charting package contains the following types of

INSIDE THE HIDDEN MARKET

---

[1] For a particularly clear demonstration of the latter, try the interactive seed-growing demonstration at www.mathsisfun.com/numbers/nature-golden-ratio-fibonacci.html.

Fibonacci indicators: arcs, fans, spirals, extensions, times series, time ratios, time extensions, and, finally, retracements. That's all well and good for the insatiable, but for our purposes, we'll follow the old KISS adage—Keep It Simple, Stupid—and restrict ourselves to only one type: Retracements.

A Fibonacci retracement measures the distance between two extremes of price—a peak and a trough—and divides that range by key ratios found in the Fibonacci series. Charting packages typically provide ratios of .236, .382, and .618 along with .50. Some packages include .786 (the square root of .618) or .784 (1 − .236). (Think indicator insatiability.) Some charting packages allow you to customize your Fibs so that you can include any ratios you would like. The measured move (MM) methodology presented in this book keeps it simple with .618, .50, −23.6, and 1.618. To see how this works, look at Figure 2.2. The trough of this price range is 1,289.07 and the peak is 1,297.53, creating a range. To create a Fibonacci retracement in this example, you would click your mouse button at the top of the peak at 1,297.53, drag the mouse down to the trough at 1,289.07, and click once more. The resulting retracement would show the levels indicated in the graphic: 100.0 percent (1,297.53), 61.8 percent (1,294.30), 50 percent (1,293.30), 0 percent (1,289.07), and 123.6 percent (1,287.07). At first glance, it might seem counterintuitive that 100 percent marks the beginning of the move and 0 percent the end point. But when viewed from the viewpoint of *retracement,* it makes perfect sense: 100 percent marks the level at which the entire move would be retraced if price moved back from the high of 1,297.53 to the low of 1,289.07. Seen in this light, it's clear that the 61.8 percent level indicates a retracement of almost two thirds of the entire move, whereas the 50 percent level indicates a retracement of exactly half the move. −23.6 percent indicates a level equal to the entire move plus 23.6 percent of the move. (Please note that in an uptrend, Fibs are drawn in the opposite direction, from low to high).

The Fibonacci retracement shown in Figure 2.2 forms one measured move. Now that it's been drawn, how should the indicated levels be interpreted? In a nutshell, as follows:

1. Price has declined from a high of 1,297.53 to a low of 1,289.07.
2. Price will probably rise from the trough of 1,289.07 to the 50 percent retracement level of 1,293.30 before resuming its downtrend to a low indicated by the −23.6 percent level of 1,287.07.

FIGURE 2.2 First Measured Move

Source: thinkorswim®. TD Ameritrade, Inc. and David Halsey are separate unaffiliated companies are not responsible for each other's services or policies. © 2014 TD Ameritrade IP Company, Inc. Used with permission. For illustrative purposes only.

3. If price does not resume its downtrend after rising from the 1,289.07 to the 50 percent retracement of 1,293.30 but instead rises to the 61.8 percent level of 1,294.30, it probably will not resume its uptrend and will rise further.

Caution: Please realize that this example is *hypothetical* and is intended for demonstration purposes only. Notice that the word *probably* is used twice in the nutshell above, reflecting the fact that the game of trading is a game of *probabilities*. No trading system is 100 percent accurate, and no trader, even the most meticulously crafted algo, is correct 100 percent of the time. All profitable traders have discovered or developed a system—a methodology—that provides them with an edge in this game of probabilities. *Trading the Measured Move* is one such methodology.

Before providing some examples of how a sequence of Fibonacci retracements can form a series of measured moves in an uptrend or downtrend and how trading those measured moves can lead to a series of profitable trades, a few definitions and a clarification are in order. Definitions first:

- *50 percent retracement, also called halfway back (HWB):* The level at which price tends to resume its upward path after retracing from the high point of a Fibonacci retracement in an up-move; conversely, the level at which price tends to resume its downward path in a down-move.

- *61.8 percent retracement, also called the failure level:* The level that, if reached, indicates price will not resume its upward path after retracing from the high point of a Fibonacci retracement in an up-move; conversely, the level that, if reached, indicates price will not resume its downward path in a down-move. In both cases, reaching the 61.8 percent level indicates that the MM has failed.

- *−23.6 percent price target:* The level marking the end point of an MM, the level at which profit taking tends to take place.

At this point a clarification must be made before moving forward. Most charting packages would present the profit target as −23.6 percent. Negative numbers! Wouldn't negative numbers indicate losses rather than profits? It certainly would appear so, but no, they wouldn't. The appearance of negative numbers as profit targets is nothing more than an artifact of the retracement drawing process. Remember that the beginning of the move is indicated as 100 percent and the end point as 0 percent. Anything beyond the end point of 0 percent is going to be represented as a negative number. But, what is this level in reality? Does the −23.6 percent level represent a loss of 23.6 percent? Obviously not. In reality, −23.6 percent represents an increase of 123.6 percent measured from the beginning of the move. If one share or contract was purchased for $100 and sold for $223.60, the resulting profit would be $123.60, or as expressed in terms of percentage, 123.6 percent. To compensate for the logical rift between label and reality, the MM methodology refers to the −23.6 percent Fib level as 123.6 percent. Most charting packages will display profit targets as negative numbers, but when reading Fib charts, MM traders pronounce the "−"s in −23.6 percent and −61.8 percent as "1"s, thereby transforming them into 123.6 percent and 161.8 percent.

■ Fibs Make the Moves

In the example displayed in Figure 2.2, we can see that price fell from a high of 1,297.53 to a low of 1,289.07 before retracing to the 50 percent HWB level of 1,293.30. Next, it bounced from 1,293.30 and continued its downward path before hitting its profit target of 1,287.07. What happened next? Remembering that we are speaking hypothetically here, take a look at Figure 2.3 to see how the successful completion of one MM can lead to the beginning of a series of interlocking measured moves. This particular example demonstrates a series of down-moves that becomes a downtrend; a similar process in reverse would result in a series of up-moves that becomes an uptrend.

Whenever price successfully completes one Fibonacci retracement from trough to high to 50 percent retracement to −23.6 percent profit target, a new Fib is drawn to project the next measured move. One MM has completed, the next is about to begin. In Figure 2.3, notice that the new Fib begins with

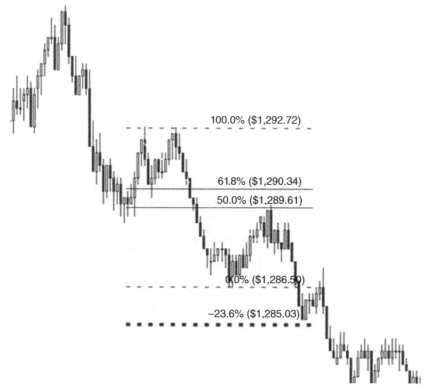

FIGURE 2.3 Second Measured Move
Source: thinkorswim®.

the point at which price retraced in the first MM: 1,292.72. This point marks the new peak. The new trough is marked by the first MM's −23.6 percent profit target at 1,286.55. Given these new 100 percent and 0 percent levels, the remaining levels of the new Fib are 61.8 percent (1,290.34), 50 percent (1,289.61), and −23.6 percent (1,285.03). Before moving to the next paragraph, look at Figure 2.4 and answer this question: to which level will price retrace before continuing its downward movement in the new MM?

1,287.51 is the correct answer because it represents an HWB retracement from the new high of 1,289.76. In our ideal example price would retrace from that level and attain a new low at the −23.6 percent level of 1,284.20, thereby successfully completing the third MM in what is now a downtrend. Another new Fib, this one projecting a third MM, would be drawn from a high of 1,289.76 to a low of 1,285.26 (see Figure 2.4). If this third MM were to complete successfully, price would retrace from 1,287.51 before reaching its −23.6 percent profit target of 1,284.20. But what if it didn't?

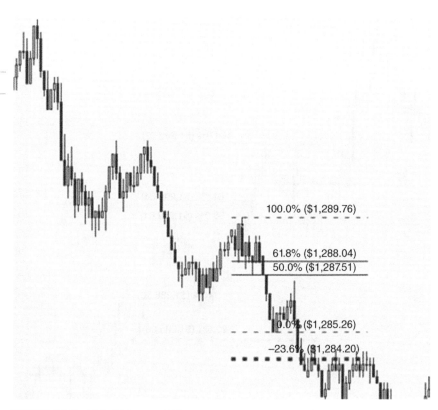

FIGURE 2.4 Third Measured Move
Source: thinkorswim®.

All traders know, or should know, that nothing goes up or down forever. All trends fail, it's a basic fact of life. In the MM methodology, failure is defined by one thing and one thing only: the 61.8 percent retracement level. To wit, if price retraces beyond the HWB 50 percent level and touches the 61.8 percent line, that Fib has failed. The significance of that failure—the failure of one single Fib—varies in magnitude depending on the context in which it occurs. For example, if the Fib underlying the sixth MM in a long uptrend or downtrend fails, that failure carries considerable significance and indicates that the entire trend has failed. At the other end of the spectrum, if the Fib underlying an MM in a sideways market in which price is barely moving fails, that failure carries a relatively low level of significance. Numerous real-world examples in this book will make these distinctions of significance abundantly clear.

Returning to our hypothetical example, Figure 2.5 shows the failure of the nascent downtrend that originated in Figure 2.2 and began to develop in Figures 2.3 and 2.4. After reaching a low of 1,280.79, price retraced HWB

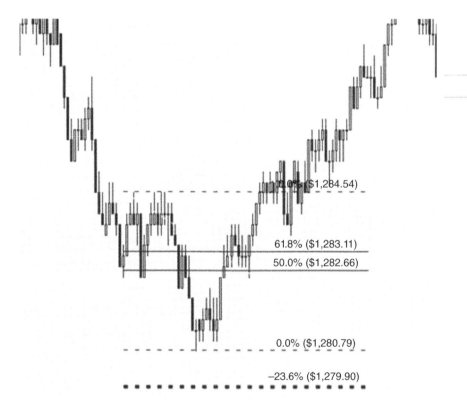

FIGURE 2.5 Measured Move Failure
Source: thinkorswim®.

to 1,282.66 but did not retrace downward. Instead, it continued rising to the 61.8 percent level of 1,283.11, which, once touched, indicated the failure of this fourth MM. It appears that our nascent downtrend didn't really have a chance to develop in full. The real world is full of similar scenarios.

Before moving on to the next section, we should look at one example of a measured move to the upside after a failure. Figure 2.6 shows a move that is the mirror image of the move in Figure 2.2.

The size of the move is exactly the same, but the direction is its polar opposite. Instead of drawing the Fib from high to low, it is drawn from low to high. Its interpretation is also the opposite of the one offered earlier for Figure 2.2.

1. Price has fallen from a low of 1,280.76 to a high of 1,285.25.
2. Price will probably fall from the high of 1,285.25 to the 50 percent retracement level of 1,283.00 before resuming its uptrend to a high indicated by the −23.6 percent level of 1,286.31.

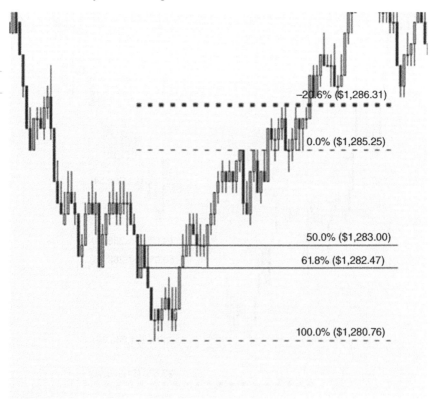

FIGURE 2.6 Next Measured Move after the Trend Failure
Source: thinkorswim®.

3. If price does not resume its uptrend after falling from the 1,285.25 high to the 50 percent retracement of 1,283.00 but instead falls to the 61.8 percent level of 1,282.47, it probably will not resume its uptrend and will fall further.

Just as the example in Figure 2.2 was extended in Figures 2.3 and 2.4 in a hypothetical series of three measured moves, Figure 2.6 could be extended in similar fashion but to the upside.

■ Why Do Fibs Work?

In the discussion of Figures 2.2, 2.3, 2.4, 2.5, and 2.6, you might have noticed that no reasons were given for any of the price movements up or down—they simply moved as if on demand. That's because we were speaking hypothetically in a world of ideals, simplifying for the sake of demonstration. In the real world, things are rarely this simple. For example, prices frequently bounce from HWB levels, but not always. Sometimes they bounce on the first touch, sometimes on the second, sometimes on the third. Sometimes they bounce from the exact HWB level to the penny or the pip or tick, sometimes from a level close to HWB as if HWB is a zone of levels rather than an absolute level. Sometimes prices don't bounce at all from HWB but continue on to the next level. Similar lists of "sometimes" apply for all of the other Fib levels as well. That being said, experience has shown that Fib levels work more often than not. Put another way, when prices approach specific Fib levels they display consistent behavior to a high degree of probability. Why is this so?

Let's take HWB first. HWB, remember, is not a real Fib level. As a ratio of 50 percent it doesn't apply to the Fibonacci series at all, except when the third number in the series is divided by the fourth, a trivial anomaly in the context of an infinite series. Its use in standard Fibonacci retracements stems from something else entirely: it's easy for humans to use. From time immemorial, from the days of Livermore and Wyckoff at the turn of the twentieth century, and most likely for many generations before that, traders have been using a 50 percent retracement as a good place to buy if going long or to sell if going short. It makes perfect sense. Imagine you are standing on a trading floor surrounded by a crowd of other traders. Price of a given instrument had steadily risen from the market open to the 30-minute mark. The mood is buoyant, the momentum bullish. However, you are not yet part of the move. For whatever reason, you have been hesitant to jump in, and from experience you realize that price will probably retrace after reaching a temporary high. As it turns out, this is exactly what happens. At the 30-minute mark, price reaches a high and begins to retrace. Over the next 15 minutes it falls to a level midway between the opening price and the 30-minute high. The market is HWB, and you realize it because it was easy for you to calculate HWB in your head with some easy arithmetic. This is your signal to buy for the next move up, so you buy at the ask (also called the offer). You are not alone; others were waiting for the same moment to buy. The aggregate volume of a large number of traders buying creates renewed movement of both the bid and ask prices to the upside. This time you're in the move.

Renewed price movements from HWB levels on a trading floor are one thing. Why does HWB work in the electronic global village of today? Does it just work because it works? In some very simplistic sense the answer is probably yes, it works because it works. At a deeper level, however, the answer most likely lies in the realm of cultural continuity, collective memory, or of something known as the meme (from *Mneme*, the ancient Greek muse of memory). Just as genes transmit biological information from generation to generation, memes are said to transmit ideas from generation to generation. Of course, no one has ever seen a meme or has proven its existence. The idea of a meme, though, is a powerful one, useful for considering the efficacy of HWB in trading. It's as though there is an HWB meme that has worked its way through human history into the trading patterns of both human and machine traders of today.

What about −23.6 percent? Why does price so often recoil from the −23.6 percent level after resuming its momentum from an HWB bounce? Just as with HWB, the answer to this question cannot be unequivocally precise. What can be asserted with confidence, however, is that the −23.6 percent level is frequently the level at which substantial profit-taking takes place. In an uptrend, it is the level at which substantial selling is often made clearly visible by a rather rapid decline in price. Conversely, in a downtrend, it is a level at which price often begins to rise rapidly in response to substantial buying of traders covering their shorts.

And finally, let's look at 61.8 percent, the level indicating the failure of a measured move. What is it about 61.8 percent that screams failure? Well, it doesn't scream exactly; it warns. On time frames ranging from minutes to weeks or even months, a touch of the 61.8 percent line frequently signals that a reversal in price direction and momentum is imminent. A clue as to why this is so could lie in its close proximity to HWB. Recall from the HWB scenario that HWB is frequently the level at which traders enter or reenter a prevailing trend. In that scenario, substantial buying occurred and price continued on its merry way upward. But what would have happened if substantial buying had not occurred and price had not bounced into a continuation of the original trajectory upward? What if price continued to fall? Two plausible outcomes come to mind without too much difficulty:

1. As price continued to fall from HWB, traders who bought at HWB expecting others to join in found themselves alone, and felt increasingly so as price continued to drop while their potential losses continued to rise.
2. As price continued to fall, HWB traders who were long from earlier lower levels found their potential profits sinking with each tick downward.

In both of these scenarios, the question is: what to do? The likely answer is bail, sell. For the trader long from below, sell in order to gather as much profit as possible before the potential is wasted further. For the trader long from above, sell in order to cut losses short. The next question for each is: which level indicates an appropriate level to sell? Experience has shown that for many traders, that level is marked by the 61.8 percent level on a Fibonacci retracement.

■ Fibs in the Real World

The MM methodology defines two basic Fibonacci types: traditionals and extensions. Each is drawn in exactly the same way except for one significant difference: the starting point from which it is drawn. Determining that starting point with precision is crucial in trading MMs successfully. After describing and explaining a few clear examples of each Fib type in action, we will examine starting point selection in depth. We will also look at ways in which sets of traditionals (or traditionals and extensions) across multiple time frames can nest inside each other like dolls of different sizes in a Russian babushka doll.

Figure 2.7 shows an example of a traditional Fib working to near perfection on a 60-minute chart of the E-mini Standard & Poor's (S&P) 500 Index futures contract, known by its symbol ES. Each candlestick represents a 60-minute increment of time. Adding the candles in this MM together, you can see that it completed in just over 52 hours. Prior to the starting point of the move at 1,222.33, price had fallen over an 8-hour period from a high of 1,249.16, setting the stage for the move back up. From a low of 1,222.33,

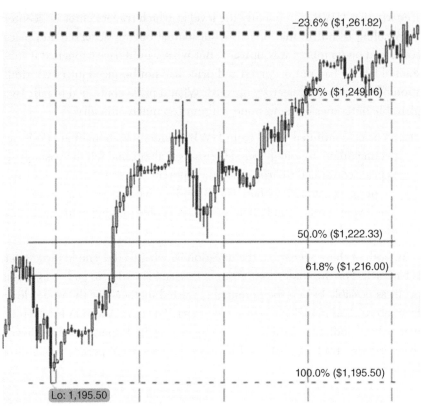

FIGURE 2.7 Traditional Measured Move
Source: thinkorswim®.

price moved up to a peak of 1,261.82, a move of 38.5 points. A 60-minute chart does not allow us to determine the exact moment at which price hit its peak, but we can see clearly that the peak was attained sometime in the fifty-second candle from the starting point. We can also see that price closed this candle somewhat below the high point of the candle. This is our signal to draw an initial Fib from the low of 1,222.33 to the high of 1,261.82. Once drawn, we wait and watch for further confirmation that 1,261.82 will indeed hold as the peak of this move.

The next candle shows that price declined and closed at the opening price of the previous candle. It attained a high of 1,264.58, 4.5 points above our peak. In the subsequent candle, however, price does attain the peak, confirming the placement of our Fib. The next candle marks the true beginning of the price movement down, although you can see that movement was not straight down and took a full three hours to touch the 50 percent HWB level. This price behavior is the very common—in fact, it is the norm. Price rarely moves in a straight line either up or down. It tends to meander from highs to lows, from lows to highs. Although they probably weren't traders, didn't the Beatles say something about a "long and winding road"? They could have been talking about price movement in any market around the world. This MM is over; on to the next.

As noted in the previous section, MMs don't always complete by reaching their targets; sometimes they fail. Figure 2.5 shows one such failure on the ES; this one, drawn from a high of 1,284.54 to a low of 1,280.79, reached 11 candles after the starting point. From that low, price rose in relatively orderly fashion to HWB, where it broke above HWB and subsequently bounced up, closing the candle at its highest level. Over the next four candles, price barely broke through the previous peak level marked by the 100 percent line before immediately plummeting, creating a clear "M"-shaped pattern. Its descent was so determined that HWB offered very little resistance as it continued its path well past the 61.8 percent failure level. As explained above, MM methodology defines a break of the 61.8 percent line as the failure of a measured move. In this particular case, there is corroborating evidence supporting the verdict that this MM has failed. First, the −23 percent target was not reached after price bounced from HWB. Second, the velocity with which price moved down through both HWB and 61.8 percent was very rapid. Added together with the fact that 61.8 percent was not just touched but violated aggressively, failure is written all over this chart. Subsequent failed attempts to rise back above 61.8 percent sounded final taps for this MM. So where do we go from here? Figure 2.6 points the way.

The MM failure depicted in Figure 2.5 demonstrates the precursor to one of the most important patterns in the MM methodology: Trend Change after Failure. Frequently, after an extended move to the downside, a failure such as the one in Figure 2.5 signals that a change in trend is imminent. (The mirror image of this pattern is seen after an extended move to the upside.) In the case of Figures 2.5 and 2.6 taken together, an MM trader who saw the failure in Figure 2.5 would draw a new Fib in the opposite direction as soon as one became visible. The profile of this new MM was revealed when a low of 1,280.76 was touched before price began retracing higher. At that point, a new Fib was drawn from the 1,280.76 low of the previously failed MM in Figure 2.5 to the new high at 1,285.25. After drawing the new Fib in Figure 2.6, an MM trader would wait and watch for price to retrace to HWB, in this case to 1,283.00. As it happened, price didn't quite make it back to full HWB but came very close before immediately beginning its rise towards its −23.6 percent target. This "close, but not exact" behavior is the rule, not the exception, in MM trading. Fib levels should be thought of as zones rather than as absolute levels. Later in the book, we will look into the topic of zones and describe effective tactics for trading them.

After price reached HWB in Figure 2.6, it meandered toward its −23 percent target over the next 11 candles. Obviously, it wasn't in too much of a hurry to get there, but get there it did. At this point, an MM trader who entered the trade long near 1,283.00 would take profit by closing the position. After profit taking, he or she would wait and watch for a new MM opportunity to develop into the beginnings of a potential uptrend. A preliminary Fib could be drawn long from the previous HWB that was bought at 1,283.00 to the high of 1,286.31 in the last candle on the chart. At this point, it is not clear whether price might begin a retrace back up or might continue to new highs. Therefore, waiting and watching is all that is called for.

Before moving on to the MM depicted in Figure 2.8, some groundwork needs to be laid. First, a basic truism: markets set up in a series of measured moves and continue in a trend of either rising or falling price until the series

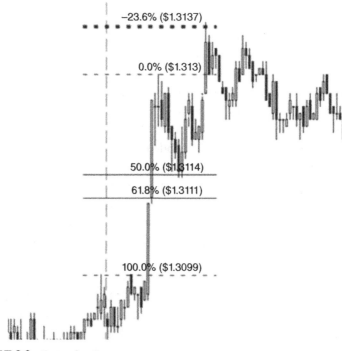

FIGURE 2.8   **Extension Long**
Source: thinkorswim®.

of MMs fails. Typically, such a series might consist of five or six MMs trading successfully from their starting points to their −23.6 percent targets. As each one completes, the next is drawn from the wherever price bounced near HWB of the completed MM to wherever price began to retrace from near its −23.6 percent target. As mentioned earlier, price rarely bounces or retraces from a Fib level *exactly*; even more rare is a bounce from an exact HWB level *and* a retrace from the exact corresponding −23.6 percent level. Both happen, but not very often. In any case, *all* series of MMs fail eventually, at which point a change in trend occurs, also known as a price reversal.

The MM series described in the last paragraph assumed a series of traditional MMs trading to completion before the last in its series failed, thereby signaling a trend change and a reversal of price direction. This is one way a series can unfold, but there are others. The vast majority of MM series begin with at least two or three MMs trading to successful completion. Sometimes, as in the last paragraph, a series will continue in traditionals for its entire duration before it fails. At other times, a striking variation can occur in which a series of traditionals is followed by a related series of extensions. As mentioned earlier, extensions are structured identically to traditionals with one major difference: their starting points.

Figure 2.8 shows an example of this second type of MM Fib, the extension, completing its excursion to its −23.6 percent profit target. Notice that the structure of this Fib is identical to the structure of the Fibs in Figures 2.5 and 2.6: each has levels of 100 percent, 61.8 percent, 50 percent, 0 percent, and −23.6 percent (not shown on Figure 2.6, but it's there). But then look at Figure 2.8's starting point: it doesn't start at a recent low but instead at a recent high! At first glance, this might seem somewhat strange. Explanation is in order.

Sometimes markets move slowly, almost gently. At other times, they move with great force and determination. It is in this latter case that the extension comes into play. Whenever price blows past its −23.6 percent target, an MM has left the domain of traditionals and moved into the domain of Extensions. Therefore, the next MM in the series will be drawn from the *high* of the last move, not from at or near its HWB level. The Fib in Figure 2.8 is drawn in exactly this way, from the previous high of 1.3099 to the next high of 1.3130. As can be seen on the chart, from this new high price retraced to HWB, the market bounced twice, and continued on to its −23.6 percent profit target. This is a clear example of a real-world extension trading to its target with near perfection.

■ In Summary

We close this chapter with another truism that will be demonstrated over and over later in this book: when extensions fail, trends fail. Once more, with emphasis: *When Extensions Fail, Trends Fail*. For now, commit this truism to memory—it is one of the most powerful aspects of the MM methodology. An equally important corollary is: *A Trend Failure Leads to the Next Series of Trades*. The importance of these two truisms cannot be overstated.

CHAPTER 3

Drawing a Road Map

Finding Direction

A career in trading can be seen as one long journey made up of a series of shorter journeys. And what are journeys without maps? Ultimately, they are journeys that most likely will not reach their desired destinations. We'll discuss personal attributes and attitudes that can lead traders to profitable destinations over the long haul. In this chapter, we'll look at maps to be used for the innumerable journeys within that much longer one. Let's hit the road and get started.

Successful traders make their way through markets by identifying trends, continuations of trends, and trend failures. Charts provide indications— clues—about the underlying road map being traveled by a given market. At any moment, the road taken by that market in the past is clearly visible. The right edge of the map leading to the future, however, is not clear at all. In fact, it is invisible. It is your job as a trader to analyze the road taken by your market thus far and to plot your own course on the road that lies ahead. Even though this might seem like driving blindly into the future, it isn't really, if you do your job well. By studying and analyzing the road behind you, you can develop strategies and tactics for navigating the future with confidence.

■ A Mountain Range of Price

A picture's worth a thousand words, right? We've all heard that a thousand times. In trading, as in many other areas, it's true. Our charts paint pictorial records of where markets have been, of how price has moved over time. Each chart provides a clear, unequivocal graphical image of a given market's price history—a map, as it were, to the past. Often, these maps display contours very similar to those of a mountain range. Therein lies a powerful metaphor useful for visualizing two crucial, interrelated market fundamentals: trends and countertrends. Merriam-Webster defines *trend* (as a noun) as "... a line of general direction or movement." For *trend* as a verb, it offers "... to extend in a general direction: follow a general course <mountain ranges *trending* north and south>." For that last part we could substitute "... market prices *trending* up and down. ..."

Figure 3.1 shows a weekly chart of one of the most powerful trends in market history: the decline of the E-mini Standard & Poor's (S&P) 500 Index

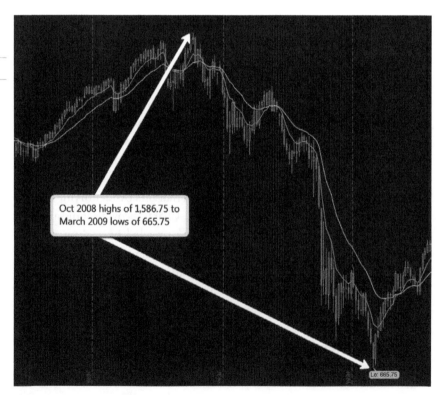

Oct 2008 highs of 1,586.75 to March 2009 lows of 665.75

Lo: 665.75

FIGURE 3.1   The 2008 Sell-Off
Source: thinkorswim®.

(ES) from the October 11, 2007, high of 1,586.75 to the November 21, 2009, low of 665.75. Anyone who was watching U.S. equity markets in those days will remember this well. (The ES actually hit a low of 665.75 on March 6, 2009, but we'll get to that later). This stunning chart invites analysis upon analysis upon analysis through any and all existing technical tools, but we'll confine ourselves here to the use of Fibonacci-based measured moves (MM) focused on the task of identifying both trends and countertrends. For our purposes, a countertrend is simply a trend in the *opposite* direction within a prevailing longer-term trend.

One trend on this chart that nearly jumps off the page is the clear downtrend from its high of 1,586.75 to its low 15 weeks later at 1,255.50. The road traveled over this range of price action was not particularly smooth or straight, but its downward trend could hardly be clearer. Once the stopping point of 1,255.50 was reached, however, strong upward countertrends developed. This development would not have surprised an MM trader because an upward countertrend toward halfway back (HWB) is exactly what should have been expected after the low of 1,255.50. Past this point on the road, however, price movement took its sweet time actually hitting HWB. From there, price retraced to full HWB over a six-week period before continuing in its downtrend and completing its profit target.

One way to characterize this type of trend/countertrend interaction in the context of mountain driving is through the example of switchbacks. Encarta defines *switchback* as: "… to form or move in sharp turns in alternating directions while going uphill or downhill." When viewing price as a moving vehicle on a mountain road, the MM trader should expect switchbacks and should be watching out for them at critical junctures. One of these critical junctures, perhaps the most significant one, is our old friend HWB, which can act as both support and resistance. For a really good example of the strength of HWB as a price level, take a look at the line marked "HWB" in Figure 3.2. Notice how often price bounces from or hovers close to this line from its first touch of support. Finally, the retouch of resistance is followed by others in the next three candles over a period of four full weeks before falling away. That's a powerful and long-lasting level.

Figure 3.3 presents another example of a very strong HWB level, this one a special case called "all the way halfway back" (ATWHWB). The MM shows the entire extent of the decline in the S&P market index as mirrored by the ES futures contract from October 2007 to March 2009, a period of almost one and a half years. Even a cursory glance at the price action

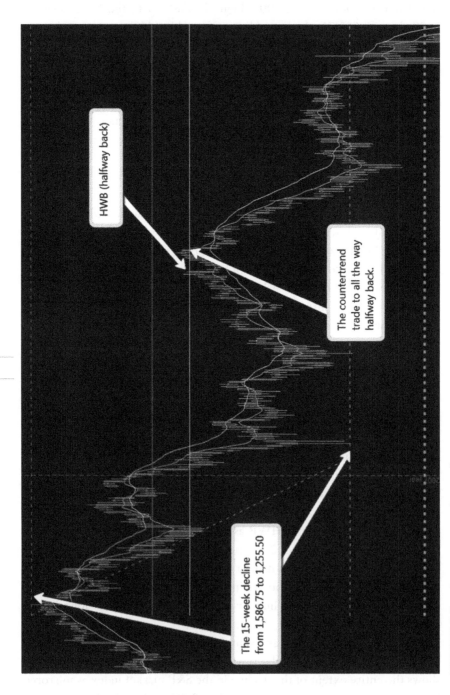

The 15-week decline from 1,586.75 to 1,255.50

The countertrend trade to all the way halfway back.

HWB (halfway back)

FIGURE 3.2 The Countertrend Toward HWB
Source: thinkorswim®.

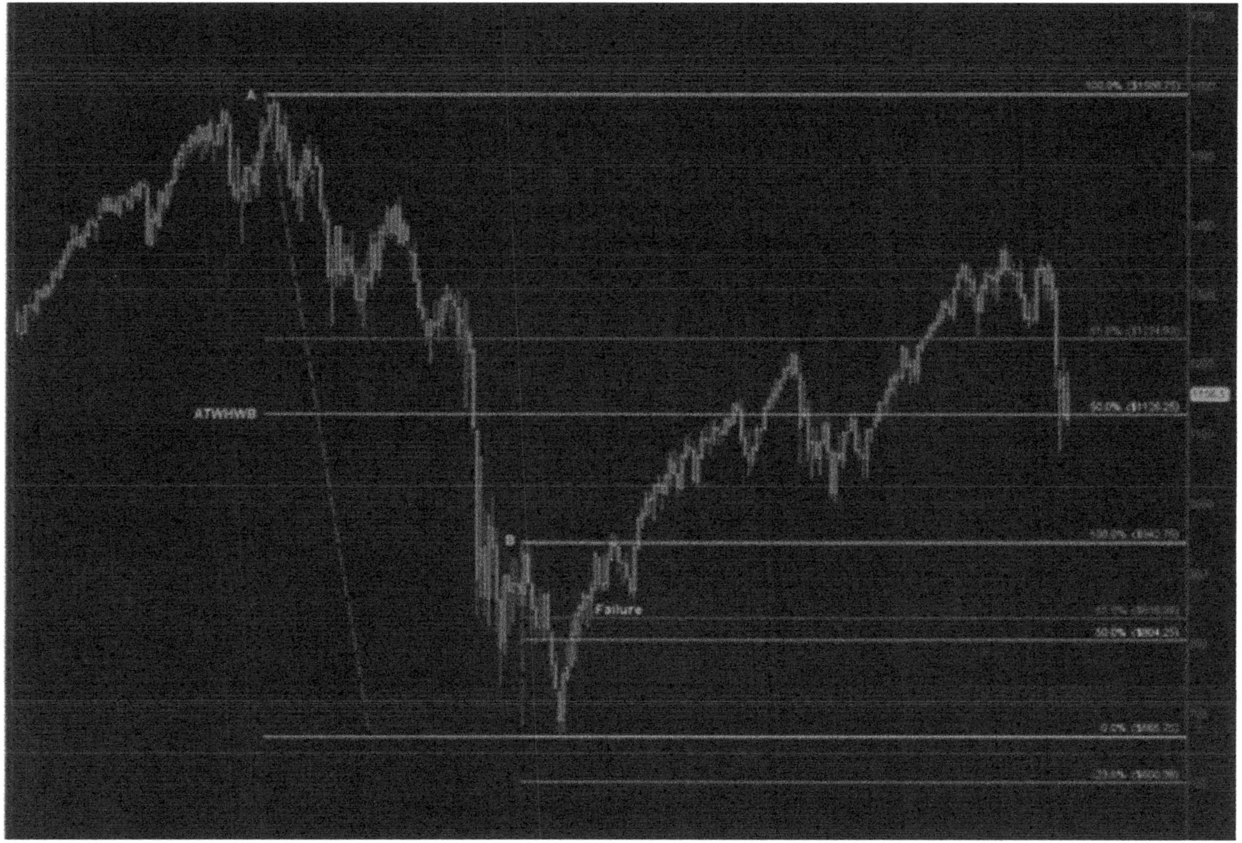

FIGURE 3.3 The All the Way Halfway Back (ATWHWB)

Source: thinkorswim®.

between those two dates shows clearly that the market declined precipitously (some would say crashed). Whatever verb or verb/adverb combination we use to describe it, the proof is in the pudding of a 58 percent price decline. Over that 17-month period the market had attempted to regain upward momentum numerous times and had failed each time. The trend had been down, down, down. However, a sea change of trend occurred just after the 665.75 low was reached, one that led to one of the greatest trend reversals in market history. The rebound began when the market failed to reverse lower at its 804.25 HWB and instead broke through its 837 61.8 percent failure level with very little hesitation. As the last short MM in a long and virtually unbroken series of short MMs, the failure of the 61.8 percent level invoked the MM axiom known by the acronym ATWHWB: whenever a trend of extended duration breaks, price can and usually does retrace all the way halfway back of the *entire* move.

In this particular case, that ATWHWB of the entire move level is 1,126.25. Notice price reaction from late December 2009 to September 2010, when ATWHWB was touched and breached many times, sometimes as support and other times as resistance, before aggressively breaking through to the upside in late September 2010. Also, notice how price reacted to ATWH-WB in the market swoon of summer 2011.

As stated at the beginning of this chapter, successful traders make their way through markets by identifying trends, continuations of trends, and trend failures. Let's look into some techniques for identifying them when they appear. We've already seen isolated examples of trends, countertrends, and trend failures in Figures 3.1 and 3.2. The examples that follow present a more extended view of each in conjunction with the others.

■ Obstacles in the Road: Pivot Points

As price travels its road up and down, it invariably encounters obstacles that can hinder or redirect its path. One of these obstacles is called the *daily pivot* (DP), which can be thought of as a kind of weighted average price for yesterday's trading in an instrument or index. The fundamental formula for its calculation is: DP = (High + Low + Close) / 3. As an example, let's say that yesterday's ES high price was 1,197, its low price 1,182, and its closing price 1,191. Given these values, the DP for yesterday would be equal to (1,197 + 1,182 + 1,191) / 3 or 1,190, which is very close to the closing price of 1,191. To see how the closing price "weights" the average toward itself, consider that if we had used the formula DP = (High + Low) / 2, the result would have been (1,197 + 1,182) / 2 = 1,189.50 which is .50 further from the close. This difference, although relatively small, is significant because the DP functions not so much as a way of understanding the trading of the day that just concluded but *tomorrow's* trading. In practice, the DP acts like an attractor for price much like a magnet does for metal objects.

The preceding formula is for calculating the central pivot point only. Many traders use this one as well as a series of other calculations for additional support and resistance levels based on the DP. In MM trading, only the central DP is used for two reasons: (1) experience has shown that of the multitude of pivot levels, the DP is the most powerful attractor of price; and (2) KISS. To this last point, recall that in Chapter 2 we invoked KISS (Keep It Simple, Stupid) to explain why MM trading makes use of only one of myriad Fibonacci types. A similar point can be made here. Since the time of William of Ockham and his razor, it has been stated in a variety of ways that for any problem the simplest solution is probably the best solution. As applied to MM trading in general, this entails keeping charts clear of extraneous detail. As to the DP in particular, KISS entails using only the central DP as a trading tool.

One very important consideration regarding DP calculations on futures contracts is whether to use the THO (trading hours only) 4 P.M. ET price or the Globex 4:15 P.M. ET price for the close value. Experience has shown that while using the Globex close creates a DP that functions as a price attractor in overnight trading after the U.S. markets have closed, the DP based on the THO close is much more consistently significant during the regular U.S. market hours of 9:30 A.M. to 4 P.M. Eastern Time.

Before moving ahead with an example of a DP in action, the topic of gaps must be introduced because of the frequently strong correlation between a DP and a gap. In the most generic sense, a gap is a difference in price between a trading instrument's opening price and the closing price of the previous trading day. Gaps can be caused by any number of factors, some related, some not: major economic or political news, catastrophes of all kinds (weather-related disasters, natural disasters such as volcanic eruptions or earthquakes, large losses of human life, etc.), declarations of war, acts of terrorism, market gyrations in other parts of the world, and so on. Whatever a gap's cause, it can be of two different types: amateur or professional. The difference between the two types is related to its size and is different for each trading instrument. For the ES, a professional gap is a gap of 10 points or more; an amateur gap is a gap of less than 10 ES points. If today's ES open is 1,195 and yesterday's close was 1,185, the gap is professional. If today's ES open is 1,171 and yesterday's close was 1,176, the gap is amateur. Beyond these two definitions are two additional terms that come into play when considering gaps: gap fill and half-gap fill. A gap is said to be filled when after the open a trade executes at yesterday's closing price "closing the gap." A half-gap fill occurs when a trade executes at a price halfway between today's open and yesterday's close. So, in the case of an ES open at 1,195 after a previous trading day's close of 1,185, a trade at 1,185 would realize a gap fill; a trade at 1,190 would realize a half-gap fill.

Typically, professional gaps do not fill; instead, price continues in the same direction away from the previous trading day's close. If today's open was above yesterday's close, price continues to climb away from that close. If today's open was below yesterday's close, price continues to fall from that close. (For our purposes here, *yesterday* means "previous trading day" rather than yesterday in a literal sense to allow for weekend and holiday situations in which the previous trading day is not literally yesterday.) Amateur gaps, however, typically *do* fill either as full gap fills or half-gap fills and do so within the first hour of trading. In all cases for all fill or non-fill situations, the final determination cannot be made until the current trading day has ended. Only then can we say definitively that a gap either filled or didn't fill.

Given the basic information on DPs and gaps, we can now look at how they interact on any given trading day. First and foremost, each level—DP, gap fill, and half-gap fill—acts as a price attractor and target. The reasons for this probably lie within the realm of self-fulfilling prophecy. If traders believe that price is likely to reach a certain level, they will hold their positions until those levels are reached, at which time they will take profit. If a retail trader trading a small account takes profit at a certain level, the effect on a market as a whole will most likely be negligible. If a professional trader trading a very large account takes profit, the effect on that market will be much greater. If *many* professional traders take profit at similar targets, the effect will be greatly magnified. This phenomenon was noticed over 100 years ago by the legendary trader Richard Wyckoff (1873–1934), who wrote about what he called the composite operator. Simply stated, Wyckoff believed that price movement in any market should be viewed as the result of a single very large trader or operator, hence the term *composite*. For Wyckoff, the actions of many traders together create market movement and direction. This perspective can be applied when considering the effectiveness of DPs and gap fill levels as price attractors and targets. Because many traders base their trading strategies on them, these levels tend to both attract price movement and result in price reaction when touched.

So, at any given market open, a DP will be present and will be either accompanied or not accompanied by a gap. If only a DP is present, it will tend to attract prices toward it from wherever the market opens. If, however, a gap is also present, there will be *three* price attractors and targets: the DP, the gap fill, and the half-gap fill.

■ Navigating Trends

So far, we've seen that as a trend unfolds over a mountain range of price, it can encounter a wide variety of twists, turns, and obstacles on the road: Fibonacci retracement levels and profit targets, pivot points, gaps, countertrends, and various levels of support and resistance. These are only a few (but a *very* important few) of the many factors that can come into play in a trend's development from beginning to end. One thing that can be said for sure, however, is another truism of trading: *trends continue until they fail.* Oh, really? This statement seems so patently obvious that it's not worth stating. But stating it, believing it, and following it could not be more crucial to the success of a trader's career. Many traders, especially beginning traders, fail to recognize the validity of this truism and in so doing miss participating in trends that could have led them to profitability. They fail to follow this truism's corollary to *trust the trend and take the setups you see.* Even if they have attained a firm grasp of a trading methodology, they fail to take advantage of their knowledge because of one thing: a lack of trust. Their training has prepared them to see trade setup after trade setup develop, but they hesitate to trade the setups because of their failure to internalize the dictum: *trust the trend.* Because of that lack of trust, fear grips these traders, and time and time again they sit by idly while a trend continues without them. The starting flag has dropped but they are left standing on the starting line. Much more will be said on this topic; it was introduced now to provide a backdrop for the discussion of trends that follow in the rest of this book.

Trends come in many sizes: short-term, medium-term, long-term, and all kinds of variations thereof. One short-term trade that occurs with some regularity is known as the trend day. A trend day is a day in which a single trend, either up or down, is maintained for an entire day. A trend day in the upward direction is defined by three specific criteria (reverse for a trend day in the downward direction):

1. Professional gap up
2. Positive breadth
3. Positive tick divergence

The first criterion was previously defined; the second and third require some attention here. As with many, if not most, technical indicators available to traders today, breadth is one that can be expressed in many different ways, some of them quite arcane. In MM trading, KISS dictates that a very simple, clear, and direct form of breadth be used, one for New York Stock Exchange (NYSE) stocks and one for Nasdaq stocks. For our purposes, breadth is the ratio of the total trade volume of stocks that are increasing in price to the total trade volume of stocks that are declining in price. Stated another way, breadth is the ratio of volume in advancing issues to volume in declining issues. For example, if the volume in advancing issues on the NYSE is equal to the volume in declining issues, NYSE breadth will be expressed as 1:1. If the volume in NYSE advancers is twice the volume of decliners, NYSE breadth will be 2:1. If the opposite is true and volume in decliners is twice the volume in advancers, NYSE breadth will be −2:1. Exactly the same math applies to Nasdaq breadth. In both cases, breadth can be viewed as an expression of market sentiment for a market as a whole. Positive breadth ratios indicate a bullish sentiment; negative ratios indicate bearishness. Very large positive breadth ratios indicate extreme bullishness; very large negative breadth ratios indicate extreme bearishness. MM trading uses both NYSE breadth and Nasdaq breadth for a more nuanced view of market sentiment. In general, NYSE breadth represents a more broad-based view of sentiment toward the business outlook for major U.S. corporations, while Nasdaq breadth represents sentiment toward the more technology-centric sectors of the U.S. economy.

Remember our old friend tick, the one that represents the number of trades per bar on a tick chart? Well, when we talk about tick divergence, we're not talking about our old friend, we're talking about one of the other ticks. Specifically, we're talking about NYSE tick. If you'll recall, NYSE tick is a number equal to the difference between the number of stocks on the NYSE that traded up in price over a specified amount of time and the number that traded down. It is a measurement of bullishness or bearishness in the market at any given time. A high positive number indicates bullishness, and a low negative number indicates bearishness. In the former, the higher the number, the more bullishness is present in the market; in the latter, the lower the negative number, the more bearishness. A 1,000 NYSE tick value is considered extremely bullish; a −1,000 value indicates extreme bearishness. But wait! The fact that NYSE tick has increased to 1,000 from somewhere below, even far below zero, doesn't mean that bullishness is likely to continue unabated. In fact, in most cases, the opposite is true. Typically, when NYSE tick hits 1,000 or thereabouts, professional traders (many of whom are algorithms, not people) are likely to sell their day-trading positions. And when that happens, as is almost always true in any supply-and-demand scenario, substantial selling leads to lower prices and a shift in sentiment from bullishness to bearishness. For this reason alone, knowing how to read NYSE tick is one the most crucial elements in MM trading, especially when trading the ES.

For our purposes here when exploring the criteria behind a trend day, we will look at a very specific kind of tick behavior called the tick divergence. In a nutshell, a tick divergence occurs for a trading instrument whenever a new high (low) tick value for the day is reached *without* a corresponding new high (low) price for the day. When this event occurs to the high side, a positive tick divergence is in play and will remain so until a new high price is reached. Similarly, when a new low tick value is reached for the day without a corresponding new low price, a negative tick divergence is in play.

■ Long and Winding Roads

A trend day's name reveals its relatively short duration—one day. But just as Rome wasn't built in a day, most other types of trends aren't either. Some develop over a week or more, a month or more, a year or more, or even a decade or more. In MM trading, it is best to evaluate any apparent trend within the context of trends that might be in effect on longer time frames. Even when day trading trends based on candles of 15-minute increments or less, an MM trader should always take a longer view first before risking capital by hitting the buy or sell button. A good place to start the viewing is on a daily chart over a time horizon of 20 years (abbreviated as 20Y Daily). This time frame might seem overly long, but experience has shown that it isn't, while it reveals another truism of MM trading: *the longer the trend, the more powerful it is.* The reasons behind this truism can perhaps be found by way of analogies drawn from the world of science, namely from Newton's Laws of Motion and Law of Universal Gravitation.

Newton's first Law of Motion states that every object in a state of motion tends to remain in that state unless an external force is applied to it. As applied to market trends, our analogy would define the object in motion as a trend and the external force as another trend in play on a longer time frame. In a typical scenario, this might entail an uptrend as seen on a daily chart coming into contact with a downtrend on a monthly chart. The external force of the monthly downtrend could be sufficient to slow down or even reverse the daily uptrend. Scenarios like this appear frequently in cases of countertrends in one direction operating within a dominant trend in the opposite direction as seen on a longer time frame. And this is where an analogy to Newton's Law of Gravitation can be applied. One of that law's tenets is that objects of greater mass carry a greater gravitational force. In the case of markets, trends on longer time frames carry more force than trends on shorter time frames. They pull price in their direction with greater force; they've got more oomph.

When day trading, the first task on an MM trader's to-do list is to look for those long and winding roads on the 20Y Daily chart. Even if the trader has drawn the same Fibonacci retracement from the same anchor for what might seem like weeks upon weeks (and really might be), the drawing should happen every single day. The primary question is: where is price in relation to the predominant trend on the daily chart? After that question is answered, the trader zooms in to the next level on a 15-minute chart, drawing one or more Fib retracements. Next question: where is price in relation to trends on the 15-minute chart? Once answered, on to the next—the micros. Whether the trader is using tick charts or time-based charts is immaterial at this point. All that matters is that the chosen chart shows price movement with a finer grain of resolution, one that feels right to the trader.

CHAPTER 4

More Tools for Trading Power

Filling the Toolbox

Any good auto mechanic is equipped with a toolbox filled with carefully selected tools in preparation for covering any and all situations that might arise. All traders should be similarly equipped and prepared. In this book, we've already seen a number of tools suited for the measured move (MM) trader: Fibonacci retracements, charts of various durations and time increments, New York Stock Exchange (NYSE) tick and the tick divergence, the daily pivot (DP), and both NYSE and Nasdaq breadth. In this chapter, we will investigate a few more tools equally suited for the critical tasks involved in trading the powerful currents of today's global markets.

39

▧ Watching the Clock (and the Calendar)

One of the most important aspects of any trading plan is to know when to trade and, probably more important, when *not* to trade. On the short list of most common mistakes made by beginning traders is the mistake of entering a trade when there is no clear and compelling reason for doing so. Many beginners feel that they've got to be "in the action" at all times or else they're not doing their job. They feel that to call themselves a trader they've got to be "in the game" at all times. Nothing could be further from the truth. The pros and the successful retail traders know better. They know when to wait. They know how to sit on their hands (SOH). They know that if a trading opportunity is not present at the moment, one will be in the future. They know the truth of this truism: *there will **always** be another trading opportunity*.

The act of watching the clock and the calendar provides an early warning system for the trader and allows him or her to forecast market conditions much as meteorologists do for the weather. A calendar provides the broad contours of likely conditions, and a clock provides finer levels of resolution. Given the enormous number of trading instruments in today's markets, a comprehensive almanac of calendar/clock data for all instruments would require numerous volumes printed in tiny typeface. Here, we will look at just a few while making the point that a trader should always be aware of specific calendar events and times of day that are likely to impact their instrument(s) of choice.

For the U.S. markets the year really begins in September. It's the end of summer, the kids are back in school, and traders are back at their desks. Historically, the last week of August shows exceptionally low volume for U.S. markets, a condition that often stretches past Labor Day until the day of the Federal Open Market Committee (FOMC) meeting in September. That day is one of eight regularly scheduled meetings held each year by the FOMC, and it is a day that is sure to see wild market gyrations, especially just after the committee releases its statement (more about that when we discuss the clock). Typically, trading activity and volume remains robust until the Christmas holidays, with a brief lull the day after Thanksgiving. The last week of December—the period between Christmas and New Year's—sees relatively low market activity. Volume usually picks back up after January 1 and remains seasonally strong until the old adage "Sell in May and Go Away" comes into play as the lazy days of summer approach. Trading activity reaches its nadir the week after July 4, when it seems that most of the major trading desks in America have been abandoned for lake cabins, golf courses, or seaside resorts.

Why should traders care about periods of low trading volume? Because low volume can often lead to unexpected market movements that don't follow typical patterns. Just as a placid lake surface suddenly pierced by a rock thrown from shore can erupt into waves of disruption, a large trade in a low-volume environment can create sudden waves of price movement seemingly out of nowhere. Here, the daily warnings of a television roll call sergeant to "be careful out there" apply equally to traders as to cops. One way to be careful in a low-volume environment is to trade at half size or not trade at all. Trading at half size means to trade half the number of contracts or shares that you normally trade. If you normally trade four contracts, trade two; if eight, trade four, and so on. Remember, not trading at all is a trade decision. Not trading doesn't mean you're not a trader, it means that you've decided to SOH until another inevitable opportunity presents itself—a *real* opportunity, not a trade just for the sake of trading.

The yearly calendar is filled with events that are likely to cause market movement in one direction or the other, way too many to mention. But here are a few to watch out for. Options expiration days occur on the Friday of the third week of each month and almost always cause periods of market movement and nonmovement. Particularly potent is the big daddy (or mommy) of them all: quadruple witching. Its little sister, triple witching, isn't too shabby, either, in its ability to cause unruly market volatility. Triple witching occurs on the Fridays in March, June, September, and December when Standard & Poor's (S&P) futures contracts, S&P 100 index option contracts, and individual stock options all expire. On these days, the last hour of trading is called the triple witching hour and is known for increased trading volume and wild price gyrations as traders unwind their positions during this hour and just before. Quadruple witching in March can be even wilder because of the addition of single stock futures contracts to the expiration list. The third week of March habitually shows very sloppy, low-volume trading until the quadruple witching hour begins to approach, at which time all heck is likely to break out. Worthy of note is this statistic: over the past 20 years the week before quadruple witching has seen upward price movement 70 percent of the time; the following week has seen downward price movement 65 percent of the time.

We live in a global village with a calendar marked in many languages. Events in one corner of the world can have an impact in another much like the proverbial flap of a butterfly wing in one hemisphere might cause a hurricane in the other. Well, maybe the butterfly/hurricane connection takes a bit too much poetic license, but you get the picture. In today's world, traders should be aware not only of FOMC meetings and statements but of European Central Bank (ECB) meetings and statements as well. And what about Jackson Hole and Davos? The former, a yearly conference of international economic leaders held in Jackson Hole, Wyoming, since 1978 has become increasingly newsworthy for global markets, especially in 2010 and 2011. Similarly, news coverage of the World Economic Forum held in Davos, Switzerland, each year is likely to impact markets as its participants issue statements and pose for photo opportunities. Traders should know when these major events are taking place and should be prepared to react to the market movements they might cause. The Internet contains a plethora of online calendars that list these and many other events that have the potential to move markets. Every trader should have one or more of these marked in his or her Favorites menu.

Some traders "trade the news." MM traders trade the *reaction* to the news. In MM trading, the content of the news is not important; it is the market's reaction to the news that is important and vitally so. Almost always it is best to SOH (sit on your hands) during a news event that is moving the market. If you're in a trade that is profitable, either exit the trade well before the news event itself or ride it out through the event as it unfolds. How did you know the news event was coming? You looked at your trading calendar, of course. If you're not in a trade, don't enter one either during the news event itself or in its immediate wake, as the market swings back and forth, often with extreme speed and vehemence. SOH and wait for a clear direction to emerge before entering a postevent trade. And always remember, be careful out there.

Before moving to the clock, let's look at the days of the week. While acknowledging that there can be special cases in which market behavior on a given day will not fit its usual pattern, each week can be divided fairly reliably into three separate personalities. Monday is the day on which the market sets direction for the week. Trading volume is most often not robust, especially in the morning. Price action is typically fairly subdued, even sluggish. In this regard, Mondays for the markets are not unlike Mondays for many workers who ease back into the workweek after a weekend full of the kinds of things people like to do on weekends. It's Tuesday when market action typically begins in earnest. Volume increases, price currents are stronger, and markets behave more "technically," meaning that price action adheres more closely to MM retracements and targets. In most weeks, this robust trading environment continues for the next two days, Wednesday and Thursday. Then comes Friday, wacky Friday. Fridays are often the days on which inexperienced retail traders give back most or all of the profits they worked so diligently to earn on the first four days of the week. Price action on Fridays is often marked by swift, unexpected spikes and dips, especially after lunch in New York. Fridays can be seen as mini-"Sell in May and Go Away" days in which institutional traders take their profits for the week by closing their positions. It's not too difficult to visualize these traders at their desks on a Friday morning after a long trading week loaded with stress levels comparable to those faced by air traffic controllers. As a long weekend in the Hamptons beckons them, the temptation to close their positions before lunch and hit the road early can understandably be too much to resist. And what happens when big positions are unloaded out of the blue? Price moves with it big time. After lunch, the trading environment can become even more treacherous because of its low volume. All of this is particularly true for Fridays before a three-day weekend when after-lunch trading can become *really* lethargic.

So what's a retail trader to do about the days of the week? How should his or her approach to trading differ depending on what day it is? Here are some good rules of thumb for your consideration: (1) trade half size on Mondays, especially in the morning after the NYSE open; (2) trade full size Tuesday through Thursday; (3) trade half size on Fridays *or not at all*. Nothing is more damaging for a trader's sense of confidence and nothing can turn a potentially great weekend into an abysmal one more than a Friday on which a winning week turns into a losing week. Nothing.

■ Tick Tock

For the MM trader, watching the clock is every bit as important as watching the calendar and perhaps more so. In the first place, knowing the day on which a given news event is likely to move the markets doesn't provide sufficient resolution for establishing trading strategies or tactics; the *time* at which the event is likely to emerge is absolutely essential. For example, FOMC announcements are almost always marked well in advance on a yearly calendar. That's good to know, but also important is that these announcements usually occur at around 2:15 P.M. Eastern Time (ET). *Very* good to know, if for no other reason than for many minutes following 2:15 P.M. ET on an FOMC day, price action, especially for futures contracts, moves like a Mexican jumping bean on steroids. Placing a winning trade during such action would be a result of nothing but pure, dumb luck. Trading during this time period is gambling, not trading.

In our present 24-hour trading environment, there are many more time zones than just the four within the continental United States to consider, especially when trading Forex or currency futures. In addition, there is a plethora of markets spread across Africa, Asia, Australasia, Europe, the Middle East, North America, and South America. Thankfully, the MM trader doesn't need to consider each and every one of them because, at present, many are too small to play a significant role in global market structure. That undoubtedly will change in the future as emerging economies in all corners of the world grow into major players, but for now there are less than 10 primary markets that we need to consider in terms of market hours. See Table 4.1 for the primary markets with their open and close times (all Eastern Time).

Careful examination of these times reveals one very significant detail: two time frames contain considerable overlap between markets: 2 A.M. to 4 A.M. for Asian and European markets and 8 A.M. to 12 P.M. for European and American markets. These two time frames, especially the latter, frequently contain levels of volume much greater than any others. And high volume most often means high liquidity and a robust, technical trading environment that lends itself to MM trading. That being said, it's important to note that particular trading instruments tend to be more affected than others by these overlaps. For example, the euro (EUR/USD or 6E) tends to be very active during the first overlap when Asia is closing and when first continental Europe opens and then London opens. That makes perfect sense because the euro is Europe's major currency—you would think that European traders would be interested in trading their own currency. One pattern that frequently emerges in this time period is a direction that started at the Frankfurt open is reversed during the London open. It happens a lot; not all the time, but a lot. *Tip:* If you're up at that hour to trade the EUR/USD pair or the 6E, be on the lookout. Another

TABLE 4.1 Open and Close Times

Market	Open	Close
Tokyo Forex	7 P.M.	4 A.M.
Hong Kong Forex	8 P.M.	5 A.M.
Frankfurt Forex	2 A.M.	11 A.M.
London Forex	3 A.M.	12 P.M.
London Stock Exchange	3 A.M.	11:30 A.M.
New York Forex	8 A.M.	5 P.M.
New York Stock Exchange	9:30 A.M.	4 P.M.
Chicago S&P Pit	9:30 A.M.	4:15 P.M.

frequent euro phenomenon occurs during the Europe/New York overlap in what is called the 11:30 reversal period. Notice that the London Stock Exchange closes at 11:30 A.M. ET and London Forex closes at 12 P.M. With a high degree of regularity, a price reversal in the euro occurs during this period as traders take their profits from a long day's trading—a European day, that is. For currency futures, this reversal period invariably leads to a currency dead zone of very little trading activity and volume beginning at 12 P.M. ET.

Another consistent pattern is extreme choppiness in the first half-hour of trading at the New York open from 9:30 A.M. to 10 A.M. One reason for this can be found in the gap fill phenomenon. Many traders trade what is called the *premarket* by "trading the gap." Traders up at that hour (for East Coasters that's 8 A.M.) often seize the opportunity to trade an expected gap fill or half-gap fill for a gap that has developed overnight or is in the process of developing in one or more of the major indices such as the S&P 500, Dow, Nasdaq, or Russell. In fact, some traders do nothing *but* trade the gap. For them, the trading day ends at 10 A.M. ET or shortly thereafter. Their trading plan involves finding a gap, placing a trade in the premarket, and waiting for their profit as the gap closes in the first half-hour of trading, or for their loss if that should be the case. The result of this gap trading, especially if done by institutional traders, is that the first half-hour of trading after the New York open is often marked by zigzag action as Big Money traders close their positions at different times, some being satisfied with a half-gap fill while others hold out for a full gap fill or somewhere in between. For a retail trader, entering a profitable trade in such an environment is extremely difficult to do. Many beginning (and not-so-beginning) traders can find themselves zigging when they should be zagging, and vice versa. For this reason, one of the rules in MM trading is to avoid trading contracts related to the major indices during the no-trade zone of the first half-hour of the New York session. The rule says, "If you're not in a trade entered in the premarket or earlier, SOH." A corollary holds that if the gap should fill before 10 A.M., the no-trade zone is no longer in effect.

Another no-trade zone or its cousin, a trade-with-extreme-caution zone, is in effect in what is known as the doldrums. What is lunchtime for New Yorkers—12 P.M. to 2 P.M.—is the doldrums for everyone else, a period of extremely lethargic trading. Many experienced traders take a nice long break during this period because they know that price action will be slow and volume low. Entering a trade in this environment is inherently very risky, much more risky than when market action is more robust. The end of the doldrums around 2 P.M., however, is a different matter. Much like the earlier reversal period around 11:30 A.M., the end of the doldrums often gives rise to another reversal around 2 P.M. A special case for this post-doldrums reversal often occurs on Mondays because many institutional traders sit out market action until 2 P.M. on Mondays, when they begin entering their large positions for the week. Being aware of these time- and calendar-related phenomena can prevent a trader from walking into a trade in the prevailing direction only to find that direction reversing in very short and decisive order. When driving on the mountain range of price, these common reversal periods are like hairpin turns on a mountain road. Watch out for them.

■ The Tape and the DOM

The legendary Jesse Livermore (1877–1940)—the one they called "The Boy Plunger" for the fortunes he made shorting the markets *before* they crashed in 1907 and 1929—was notorious for his tape-reading skills. But years before he had his own ticker-tape machine in his New York trading office, Livermore had learned to follow price action by keeping the flow of numbers in his head. Edwin Lefevre's book *Reminiscences of a Stock Operator* (John Wiley & Sons, 1922) tells the story of Livermore's life from his earliest days as a 14 year-old quotation-board boy at the Paine Webber brokerage in Boston. Young Jesse's job was to listen for customers to call out prices spit out by the ticker and to write them on a big chalkboard for all to see. He said, "(The prices) couldn't come too fast for me. I have always remembered figures. No trouble at all." He went on:

> Those quotations did not represent prices of stocks to me, so many dollars per share. They were numbers. Of course, they meant something. They were always changing. It was all I had to be interested in the changes. Why did they change? I didn't know. I didn't care. I didn't think about that. I simply saw that they changed. That was all I had to think about five hours every day and two on Saturdays: that they were always changing. (pg. 2)

Spoken like the supreme technical trader that he was, Livermore didn't think about the *reasons* for price action, only about the price action itself.

Later, when he began to place his own trades, he said, "I was playing a system and not a favorite stock or backing opinions. All I knew was the arithmetic of it." With algorithms in his heart, if Livermore were trading today, he would no doubt be a quant trader par excellence.

Today's trading rooms, of course, are not filled with the constant clatter of ticking tape machines, but instead with the glow of multitudes of monitors displaying charts of graphical contours along with columns containing a constant flow of numbers like riverbanks containing the rush of mountain snowmelt. The action is fast and furious and can seem quite intimidating for the uninitiated. Once initiated, though, this intimidation factor tends to disappear. So, let's get started by looking at the modern equivalent of the tape: time and sales (T&S).

A T&S window is offered as standard equipment in most charting packages. Actually, if a charting package doesn't offer T&S, don't even consider using it. Most T&S windows look like the one in Figure 4.1, which displays T&S for the E-mini S&P 500 Index (ES). The column is divided into three vertical sections. On the far-left edge, time is displayed in hours:minutes:seconds format. The middle section displays price, and the far-right section displays size. The purpose of the T&S window is to display each trade just after it has executed. Each entry is time-stamped with the time of execution, and includes the trade's price and the size of the trade expressed in the number of contracts, shares, or lots. In this black-and-white book, the usual color-coding of most T&S windows cannot be shown. Normally, if a trade executed at a price lower than the previous trade, it will be displayed in red; if a trade executed at a higher price than the previous trade, it will be displayed in green; if the price is unchanged, it will display with the same color as the previous trade. Thus, most T&S windows appear as constantly changing blocks of colored numbers, sometimes all green, sometimes all red, and at other times in various combinations of differently sized blocks of green and red. The size of those blocks and the rate at which they flow and change is one of the keys to successful tape-reading. In Figure 4.1, the color of each entry is indicated by green for buyer or red for seller.

Reading from the bottom Figure 4.1 shows the ES trades from 15:06:50 (Eastern Time) through the last trade on the tape at 15:09:20. The topmost entry always displays the last trade executed. When a subsequent trade is made, it pushes the last trade (and all previous) trades down one notch in the list. As a result, the trade previously at the bottom of the list is pushed off the screen. The screenshot shown in Figure 4.1 was taken after the market had closed for the day. Eighteen contracts sold at 1,785.25. Why

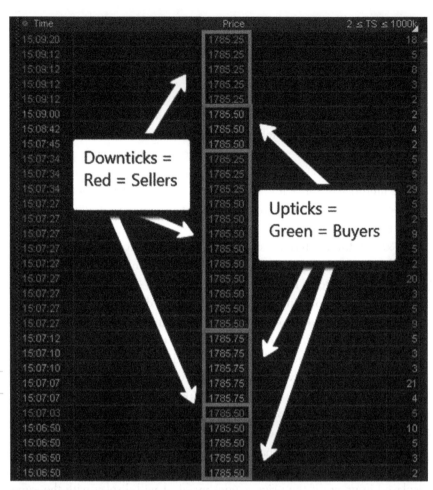

FIGURE 4.1 Time and Sales

Source: thinkorswim®.

bought and not sold? Because its color is green, indicating that the trade was executed at the offered price. The previous two trades, time-stamped 15:09:12, were sells of five and eight contracts, respectively. Looking at the rest of the trades in the list, it can be seen that more trades were red than green, indicating more selling than buying, with the sells generally being of larger size. What would that tell a trader about price action at this particular time? The conclusion is that there was more selling than buying for the ES. In and of itself, that interpretation doesn't provide sufficient information for formulating a trading strategy or tactic for the next trading day, but when considered in context with the preceding 15 to 30 minutes, it very well could.

Suffice it to say that good tape readers develop the ability to judge market speed simply by watching the rate at which trade executions flow through the T&S window. This ability is one of the tools to be used in the trade decision-making process. Here are some truisms and hints related to market speed:

■ When the market's slow, trade it slow; when it's fast, trade it fast.

■ When you have to wait 30 minutes or more for an initial profit target to be reached, you know the market is in a slow tempo.

■ When markets trade quickly, trade setups come in intervals of 7 to 10 minutes. When trading slowly, the intervals are elongated to 30 minutes or more.

■ All price movement in the markets is based on cause and effect. If the cause occurs slowly, the effect will occur slowly; if the cause happens quickly, so will the effect.

■ In slowly moving markets very quick, explosive price action either up or down is caused by market orders executing as stops are hit. In such cases, traders who "sold lows," meaning that they entered short trades near the bottom of a downtrend, are stopped out as price rises; traders who "bought highs" near the top of an uptrend are stopped out as price falls. To avoid being one of these traders, one should follow this cardinal MM trading rule: *Never* buy highs or sell lows.

■ If you see significant speed in a micro MM step back to the next larger time frame for confirmation of its place in the prevailing longer-term MM before making a trade decision.

■ The DOM (Depth of Market)

The DOM (usually pronounced with a long "O" as in an architectural dome) displays the depth of market for a given trading instrument. Also called a "ladder," a DOM shows the bid and ask prices at various levels, along with the size being bid or offered at each level. As each trade executes, a DOM indicates the price and size of the trade just after its execution.

Some traders swear by the DOM as a valuable viewing port on the market internals of supply and demand, market speed, and buying and selling pressure. MM traders see the DOM as being a place where liars play poker while simultaneously it remains one the most important tools a trader has at his or her disposal. This dichotomy demands explanation.

Liars' poker, really? Well, yes, as in any competitive endeavor, the trading playing field is a place of subterfuge, hidden agendas, and fake-outs. Football has its Statue of Liberty and fake punts, field goals, and reverses. Boxing has its feints and fancy footwork. Baseball has hidden ball trickery and a battery of deceptive hand signals, and so on. Traders, especially Big Money traders, have a few tricks of their own. One of them is to "flash the DOM" by entering a big trade to either buy or sell at a price away from the current best bid and ask prices and then pulling the order very quickly before there is any possibility of its actually executing. Their purpose, nefarious as it might be, is to lure unsuspecting traders into buying or selling based on the (mistaken) belief that Big Money will be buying or selling big very soon. Today's HFT traders have honed this kind of trickery into a high art of blinding speed and in the process placed enormous demands on the carrying capacity of the world's global electronic trading networks. So far, the networks seem to be coping, but stay tuned as more and more institutions move deeper and deeper into algorithms of all kinds. In this treacherous environment, the retail trader should always heed the warnings of that TV roll call sergeant who said at the beginning of each and every episode, "Be careful out there." In the context of DOM watching, that translates to "don't believe that unusually large bids or offers on the DOM are what they appear to be because they probably aren't."

If it's true that the DOM is a place where deception and trickery are rampant, then what's it good for? In conjunction with a sophisticated order-entry system, the DOM shines as an efficient means of trade order entry and management. While the physical appearance of DOMs can vary from broker to broker and is usually just a matter of relatively trivial cosmetic differences, the methods by which they interact with a broker's system of order entry, stop placement, and target selection is of utmost importance to the MM trader. In fact, it cannot be stated strongly enough that the absence of a sophisticated DOM in a trader's toolkit constitutes an extreme impediment to that trader's profitability and success. Without it, trading would be like approaching the task of moving a boulder with two bare hands and a shovel rather than with a front-loader tractor. Like any good tool or machine, a sophisticated DOM-based order entry and management system leverages a human's ability to get the job done, in this case by automating as much of the trading process as possible. By automating stop and target placement and movement, such a system frees the trader from these essential tasks that can be so difficult to complete in the heat of the moment as a trade plays itself out. The bottom line: Get a good DOM before entering a single trade. You'll be glad you did.

■ A Full Toolkit

Well, there you have it: a trader's toolkit loaded with the precision and power tools necessary to succeed as a measured move trader. In the next chapter, we will put all of the information in the preceding chapters together into the act of actually placing and managing a trade.

CHAPTER 5

The 90 Percent Factor—Executing Your Trade

Where the Rubber Meets the Road

A lexander Graham Bell, inventor of the telephone, said it best: "Before anything else, preparation is the key to success." In that light, the first four chapters of this book serve only one purpose: to prepare you, the retail trader, for entering the markets and prospering as a measured move (MM) trader. The task is daunting and the challenges are many, but with sufficient preparation the journey to profitability is one that can be taken with confidence. This chapter shows where the rubber meets the road—order entry and trade management—and provides the keys for launching and navigating the trip ahead.

■ Priorities and Job One

There are two overriding priorities for the MM trader:

1. Achieving reduced-risk trades, and
2. Riding the coattails of Smart Money.

The remainder of this chapter will detail the rules and tactics necessary for attaining these two fundamental priorities and will address some of the reasons for their importance.

The number one priority, so important it must be called Job One, is for the MM trader to achieve free trades. Nothing is more important—nothing. Before explaining the reasons for its importance, a definition is in order. Simply stated, a reduced-risk (RR) trade is a trade in which all significant risk is taken off the table at the earliest possible time. Achieving RR trades for different trading instruments requires slightly different tactics, but generally speaking, the overall goal is the same: to reduce the amount of capital risk to nothing but commission cost and slippage as soon as possible after entry. As an example, here are the settings for stops and profit target levels for a long trade on the 6E futures contract:

Initial stop $= -12$ pips
Target 1 $= +6$ pips
Moved stop $= -6$ pips
Target 2 $= -23$ percent Fibonacci level

In order to achieve RR trades, a trader must trade multiple contracts, with two contracts being the minimum. The reason for this is implied by this cardinal rule for trading with free: *take half the position off after the first target is hit*. Assuming that this 6E trade played out to completion from an entry at 1.3590 either for maximum profit, maximum loss, or as a breakeven *scratch* trade, it would follow one of three possible scenarios.

Scenario 1: Maximum Profit

1. Two contracts bought at 1.3590
2. One contract sold at 1.3596 (Target 1)
3. Stop moved to −6 pips
4. One contract sold at −23 percent target

In Scenario 1, a free trade is achieved in Step 3 after a profit of +6 pips on one contract has been booked and the initial stop has been moved to −6 pips. The math here is really quite simple: after Step 2 this trade has a profit of 6 pips; after Step 3 its maximum potential loss is −6 pips: $+6 - 6 = 0$. In this hypothetical trade to completion, when price reaches Target 2 at the −23 percent Fibonacci level, the second contract is sold and added to the initial +6-pip profit resulting in the trade's total profit.

Scenario 2: Breakeven (Scratch)

1. Two contracts bought at 1.3590
2. One contract sold at 1.3596 (Target 1)
3. Stop moved to –6 pips
4. One contract sold at 1.3586 (moved stop)

Just as in Scenario 1, in Scenario 2 a free trade is achieved in Step 3 after a profit of +6 pips on one contract has been booked and the initial stop has been moved to −6 pips. In this hypothetical, however, the trade moves against the trader after Step 3 and the stop is executed at −6 pips. In this case, the total loss will amount to whatever the commission cost was for entering and exiting the trade in what is known as a *round trip.* If there is some slippage and the stop executes at −7 pips instead of −6, the total loss will increase by $12.50, the dollar amount assigned to each pip for the 6E.

Scenario 3: Maximum Loss

1. Two contracts bought at 1.3590
2. Two contracts sold at 1.3582 (initial stop)

In Scenario 3, this trade results in a *full stop-out* and a loss of −24 pips (12 pip stop × 2 contracts) plus commission costs. For the 6E a full stop-out of this magnitude amounts to $300 (24 × $12.50) plus commission. While enduring a full stop-out is never a pleasant experience for a trader, knowing in advance what the dollar amount of the loss would be if realized is an extremely important factor essential for that trader's trading plan. So, before entering a trade, the trader must ask…

■ What's the Risk, What's the Reward?

Calculating a risk-reward ratio should be Step Zero in every trade decision. In other words, knowing *in advance* what your maximum loss (risk) and potential profit (reward) might be for any given trade is absolutely essential before proceeding further in the trade decision and entry process. The TV advertiser's phrase "Don't leave home without it" comes to mind here. In the trader's world, no trade should be entered without both risk and reward expressed specifically in hard, cold numbers. How is this done for risk? With very simple multiplication that we all learned in school. In a trader's risk calculation, the multiplicand is a number specifying account size in dollars, for example, $10,000, $25,000, $50,000. The multiplier is a percentage, the exact size of which is open to some, but not much, discussion. Some traders believe that risking as much as 3 percent of an account on any one trade is acceptable. Others feel that no more than 2 percent should be risked. The measured move methodology holds that risk for any one trade should never exceed 1 percent of a trader's total account size. In MM trading, any risk greater than 1 percent is considered *scared money*. Trading scared money, especially in the highly leveraged futures market, does not allow traders, whether neophytes or experts, to follow the MM rules strictly, consistently, and without emotion. Why no emotion? Because in almost any activity or endeavor, emotions based on fear or greed can cause humans to act in ways that are contrary to their own best interests. This is true in spades when trading one's own money. More will be said about this later when we explore topics of trader psychology, emotional capital, and the fear/greed dichotomy.

Given the arithmetic described above, calculating the maximum risk per trade for a trader's account is very easy through this formula: Maximum Risk = Account size × .01. A trader with a $10,000 account can risk $100 per trade (10,000 × .01); a $20,000 account allows for a maximum risk of $200 (20,000 × .01); and a $50,000 account allows a risk per trade of $500 (50,000 × .01). (Commissions need not be part of these calculations). After a trader has calculated, memorized, or, better yet, *written on paper* the maximum risk that he or she can assume on any one trade, the next step of applying this risk level to specific trading instruments can be undertaken. For example, we know from the scenarios described above that the 6E carries a value of $12.50 per pip and that the maximum loss for two contracts with stops set at −12 pips is $300 (12.50 × 8 × 2). Three hundred dollars is 1 percent of $30,000; therefore, trading two 6E contracts per trade is possible for account sizes of $30,000 or more. A trader with an account of less than $30,000 would be prohibited from trading two contracts per 6E trade according to the MM 1 percent risk rule. For traders in this situation, there are two ways to trade the EUR/USD without breaking the 1 percent rule: (1) trade one contract *all-in/all-out* or (2) trade two contracts of the E-mini EUR/USD contract (ticker: E7), which at half the size of the 6E carries a $6.25/pip value. Going even further, the E-micro EUR/USD contract (ticker: M6E) carries a $1.25/pip value making multiple-contract trades possible with even less risk per pip. Recently, the CME has introduced a number of these micro contracts for popular currency pairs. Much more information on this topic can be found at www.cmegroup.com.

After calculating maximum acceptable risk, the next step in establishing a trade's risk-reward ratio is to quantify the potential reward. The formulae for calculating reward can be more complex than those for maximum risk depending on the number of contracts being traded. All-in/all-out calculations obviously will be the simplest to calculate, given that only one profit target needs to be factored in. Reward calculations for multiple contracts with multiple profit targets will be more complicated. In MM trading, one factor will always be the same whether 1 or 21 contracts are traded—a profit target will be set at the −23 percent Fibonacci level. Multicontract trades will have at least one and potentially two or more additional profit targets; all-in/all-out trades will have nothing but a 123 percent target. In all cases, a −23 percent target will be present. With that rule in mind, here are a few risk-reward calculations based on the 6E example in the previous Priorities and Job One section.

The trade in Figure 5.1 was entered long with two contracts at 1.3130, a halfway back (HWB) level based on a Fibonacci retracement drawn from a low of 1.3091 to a high of 1.3168. The −23 percent line on this Fib is

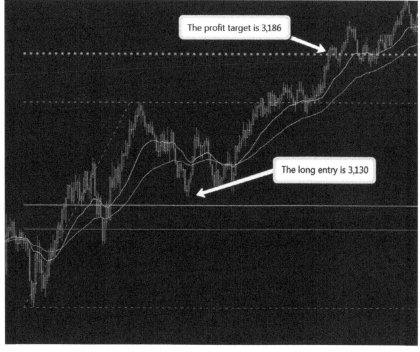

The profit target is 3,186

The long entry is 3,130

FIGURE 5.1 6E Risk Reward
Source: thinkorswim®.

1.3186. Given these values, the stop and target values listed above, and the $12.50/pip value for the 6E, the risk-reward calculations would be:

1. Initial stop = −12 pips (−12 × 2 contracts = −24 pips maximum risk)
2. −24 × $12.50 = $300 maximum risk
3. $1.3186 − $1.3130 = $0.0056 (56-pip) price differential from HWB to −23 percent profit level at Target 2
4. 56 × $12.50 = $700.00 profit for contract sold at Target 2
5. $700.00 + (6 × $12.50) = $775.00 total profit for contracts sold at Target 1 (+6) and Target 2 (+44)
6. 775/300 = 2.5:1 risk-reward ratio

Now wait a minute. That sixth step showing a risk-reward ratio of 2.5:1 doesn't look right, does it? The math is right—a maximum reward of 775 is divided by a maximum risk of 300, producing a result of 2.5. It's the name that's wrong. The correct name should be reward-risk ratio, shouldn't it? Well, yes, but not many traders call it that. For better or worse, in common practice the calculation puts reward on top, but in its name risk comes first. Actually, that's probably as it should be—in order to draw traders' attention to potential risk, something they all would like to avoid, putting risk first forces them to consider it *before* concentrating on the potential, and much more desirable, reward. As for the 2.5:1 ratio itself in this example, how should a trader interpret this relationship of reward to risk? Is it a good ratio, a bad one, or something in between? Specifically, is 2.5:1 good enough to put a trade on? While most traders undoubtedly would say the larger the ratio the better, a ratio of 2:1 is generally held to be acceptable for entering a trade. Some traders who like to ride on the wild side will enter trades with 1:1 ratios or even smaller. But in general, 2:1, 3:1, or 4:1 risk-reward ratios are widely held as worthy of trade entry. In MM trading, 2:1 is the bare minimum.

As mentioned, another essential step in evaluating a potential trade according to its risk-reward potential, is to ascertain whether a trader's account size is sufficient for taking that trade. In the case of this two-contract example, the maximum risk is $300. What is the minimum account size necessary for a per-trade risk of $300? Using MM trading's 1 percent rule—.01 × Account size = Maximum per-trade risk—the answer is $30,000 (.01× = $300; $300 / .01 = $30,000). The result of this calculation quantifies the maximum acceptable risk per trade for a trader's account size and must be so deeply ingrained in that trader's psyche that it becomes part of his or her DNA. Even though this maximum risk level is hard-coded in pure dollars and cents, the primary reason for its critical importance has a psychological component along with the financial. On the face of it, the financial impact of a 1 percent loss is actually very small, almost miniscule. If a trader has $30,000 in an account and places one losing full stop-out trade, that account balance would then be $29,700 (not including commission). In numerical terms alone, that's certainly not too big of a deal. And therein lies the psychological component. It is precisely because a 1 percent loss is "not too big of a deal" that a trader can avoid the trap of trading scared money. For a retail trader trading his or her own money, especially in the presence of the huge capital being thrown around by institutional traders from all corners of the globe, the roles of confidence and courage could not be more important. Without exaggeration, today's trading marketplace can be called cutthroat, brutal, and/or vicious (your choice) and is definitely not a place of daffodils and sweet birdsong. In order to play the game successfully, a trader needs courage and confidence. Being afraid of taking losses *cannot* be part of a trader's game plan. While it is not possible to erase *all* fear from the equation, minimizing it through careful calculation and preparation will always give the retail trader a leg up. Remember Mr. Bell's words from the beginning of this chapter and apply them. And remember this: in MM trading, any risk greater than 1 percent per trade is scared money.

Finally, for this two-contract 6E example, a $30,000 account balance would allow a trader to take the trade according to the 1 percent rule. However, if that trade resulted in a loss, it would bring the account balance below $30,000, thereby prohibiting subsequent trades, according to that same 1 percent rule. For this reason, an account balance somewhat higher than $30,000 would give a trader some maneuvering room to accommodate a few or even several losing two-contract trades without falling below the required account balance. Preserving financial capital is a key component in maintaining emotional capital. *Both* are essential for success in the life of a trader.

■ A Brief Pit Stop

One more thing before we move ahead to the mechanics of placing a trade: why are reduced-risk trades so important? The answer can be found in the next-to-last sentence of the previous paragraph and has two aspects. First, it should go without saying that preserving financial capital is *the* most important goal for any trader. Without cash to trade, no trades can be taken, and a trader's career is over, or at least stalled, until that capital is restored. Second, without the emotional capital, which is based in large part on preserving financial capital, a trader's life most likely will be full of anxiety and trepidation, two characteristics that will almost assuredly lead to additional depletion of financial capital, leading to further depletion of emotional capital. Do you see the downward spiral being formed? Many traders, especially inexperienced ones, hesitate to forgo the dream of huge profits by selling half of their positions early in order to achieve RR trades. What they fail to recognize is that preserving capital—keeping powder dry—is more important than huge profits in the long run. Huge profits can be tremendously exciting in the short term, but trading without reduced risk can turn those huge profits into huge losses very, very quickly. When considering whether or not to use the RR tactic, the adage "better safe than sorry" could not be more appropriate.

■ Preparing the DOM

Now that we've seen the importance of acceptable risk-reward ratios and RR trades in an MM trading plan, we can move ahead to the mechanics of order entry and trade management. After working though a few calculations like those detailed earlier, you might be asking yourself if it's really necessary to go through a six-step risk-reward calculation each and every time you place a trade. The answer is yes and no. Yes, knowing risk-reward ratios in advance is an essential component of any successful trading plan. No, the calculations need not be done again and again as trades are placed one after another. Borrowing from the ancient Greeks, who said, "Know yourself," MM traders should "know your instrument" and "know your risk-reward ratios." Putting the two together in a set of DOM order presets for each trading instrument that automate much of the trade management process will result in a set of fine tools that are both precise and powerful. Knowing yourself is important, too. For now, let's create a DOM preset for two-contract 6E trades.

At the time of this writing, experience has shown that if a trade is entered at an appropriate level, a 12-pip stop will give a 6E trade sufficient room to play itself out before hitting a +6-pip first profit target. Once again, here are the levels for the 6E listed at the beginning of this chapter, which will now be entered into a DOM preset:

Initial stop = −12 pips
Target 1   = +6 pips
Moved stop = −6 pips
Target 2   = −23 percent Fibonacci level

Any sophisticated DOM should allow for *bracket orders* in OCO format, in which the execution of one part of the order cancels the other part. It should also allow for multiple profit target specifications and for initial stops to be moved to a specified level after first profit targets are hit. One DOM's terminology or mechanics for entering or saving specific parameters might differ from another DOM's, but the functionality should be very similar, if not identical, for all DOMs. For the 6E example, the levels above would be entered for initial stop (−12 pips), first profit target (one contract at +6 pips), level to which the second contract's stop would be moved after the first profit target is hit (−6 pips), along with the number of contracts to be traded (2). Target 2 needs to be specified in terms of pips, not a Fibonacci level, so a trader would need to decide on a generic number of pips that would serve as a default for all 6E trades. In this example, let's use one contract at +25 pips for a default Target 2. Because we are configuring this preset for two-contract trades, the profit target settings will need to specify a level for each of the two contracts as we have done. In practice, a trader would adjust the default level of Target 2 if necessary after each trade entry was executed. Only in the most extreme cases of market volatility and speed would a trader not have time to adjust Target 2 before it executed. For this example, we'll assume that the +25-pip default for Target 2 happens to be at the −23 percent level, so no adjustment will be necessary.

After these settings have been entered for the 6E they would be saved as a preset for the 6E and only the 6E. Each trading instrument should have its own DOM with its own set of unique presets suited to the trading personality of each trading instrument and to the risk-reward profile of each trader. The next step in the trading process would be to invoke the DOM through a mouse click or menu command and wait for the right conditions for order entry.

■ Crossing the Starting Line

Many traders call the act of placing a trade "pulling the trigger." While that phrase does seem perfectly appropriate, in order to stay consistent with the vehicular metaphors used in this book, the phrase "crossing the starting line" will be used. To refine the point further, let's remember that MM trading is much more like a mountain road rally than a high-octane, pedal-to-the-metal race on a drag strip or oval track. It's more long-haul than sprint. And because of that, MM traders always use limit orders when crossing the starting line, not market orders. Why? Because MM traders are picky about price. They drive a hard bargain; they are tough negotiators. When MM traders see a measured move begin to develop, they wait until a low and a high have been clearly established. They know that until these lines of demarcation have been firmly established, conditions are not right for defining a measured move by drawing a Fibonacci retracement. Once conditions are right and a Fib has been drawn, they wait again, this time for retracement to HWB. But this period of waiting is not merely passive. Once HWB has been identified, a limit order can be placed at or near that level. All of the preparation has been done, the starting line can be crossed, the order can be been entered.

In Figure 5.1, the 6E order would be placed at 1.3130. At this point, because the DOM has been configured to *automatically* place stops and profit targets and to move stops after the first target has been hit, the trader's job is done for now. Price either will reach the limit order level and trigger the order's execution or it won't. If the trade does execute, the trader's job is to sit back and watch the trade play itself out. To recap, the multiple processes for order entry detailed so far can be encapsulated in three simple steps:

1. Calculate risk-reward ratio.
2. Place limit order with DOM preset.
3. SOH (sit on hands), wait for the order to fill, and allow the trade to play itself out.

In this chapter's first section, we saw three possible scenarios for how this trade might play itself out. Let's look at how these scenarios would play out inside the DOM. First, for maximum profit:

1. Limit order executed for two contracts bought at 1.3130, stops for both contracts placed at 1.3118 (−12 pips), Target 1 placed at 1.3136 (+6 pips), Target 2 placed at 1.3155 (+25 pips).
2. One contract sold at 1.3136 (Target 1), stop for first contract canceled, and stop for second contract moved to 1.3124 (−6 pips).
3. One contract sold at 1.3155 (Target 2), stop canceled.
4. $12.50 × (6 + 25) = $387.50 profit before commission

All four of the steps in this scenario executed automatically because the DOM was preconfigured to do so. Once the trade was entered at 1.3130, no further intervention was required by the trader. *This is how to do it!* That's easy to say or to write but not so easy to do. The number one mistake made by inexperienced traders is overtrading, and overtrading is a very easy trap in which to fall. Usually, overtrading is thought of as placing too many trades over a given time frame, and doing so definitely can be a problem for many traders. The type of overtrading addressed here is a different one but can carry equally insidious effects. It involves the *many* temptations that lie in wait for traders after orders are executed. It's so easy to move stops away from initial settings if price approaches a full stop-out at levels a little too close for comfort. It's just as easy to exit the trade early before Target 2 is hit. To succumb to either temptation requires nothing more than a quick click-drag-and-drop with the mouse. Yielding in this way, however, can lead a trader into a pit of quicksand that can be extremely difficult to escape. Let's address each temptation separately.

The most common cause for moving stops away from initial settings can be found in a trader's inability to "take the heat." Once the starting line has been crossed and the trade order has executed price can do one of three things: remain at entry level, move away from entry in the trade's favor, or move against the trade. The first possibility is rare in active markets and most often occurs only in periods of relatively sluggish market motion. The second possibility, obviously, is the one all traders hope for and is the one that is less likely to engender feelings of fear. But it doesn't always happen that way. Most traders would say that the third possibility is the norm rather than the exception. More often than not, price moves against the trade before it hits either Target 1 or triggers full stop-out. Sometimes that period of time is very short, and at others it can be very long. That's quantitatively speaking. For many traders, *any* time underwater can seem inordinately long, much longer than its actual clock time. Enduring both of these aspects of time underwater—real clock time as well as perceived time—is called "taking the heat." The ability to take heat comes easier to some traders than to others. Whereas some seem to have been born with it, for others it is a skill that must be developed. In all cases, a successful career in trading cannot be achieved without an ability to take heat. So, if you're not born with it, how do you develop it?

One way to develop heat-taking skills is through the disciplined use of trading rules. In MM trading the use of a preconfigured DOM is one very useful tool to that end. In the example above, one that led to maximum profit, the four listed steps make it appear that the trade moved from entry in Step 1 to Target 1 in Step 2 in a straight line up. But what if that weren't the case? What if in between Steps 1 and 2 price declined to 1.3123 or even to 1.3119? What if it did this not once but several times in an oscillating movement down, up, and back down again? How would those price oscillations make the trader feel? A dip to 1.3123 might feel one way whereas a dip to 1.3119—1 pip away from full stop-out—might feel, would probably feel, very differently. A multitude of factors could come into play here regarding the amount of heat a trader might feel in such a scenario. Personal issues, trading experience, life events, the won/loss ratio of x-number of preceding trades, you name it. The point here is that heat is relative and will be felt differently by each individual. What is constant, though, is that the disciplined use of a preconfigured DOM can give an MM trader a leg up in dealing with that heat, in taking it. When an MM trader preconfigures a DOM for each of his or her trading instruments the trader should make a commitment to allow that DOM to take over the trade after entry. Stops set to specific level should be allowed to trigger if hit. No intervention by the trader is necessary or desired. A rule is a rule. Strict adherence to trading rules leads to profitability. For MM trading, these points cannot be overstated.

Continuing the scenario for this trade in which considerable heat was generated by repeated dips to very near full stop-out, consider the impact of Target 1's being hit. At that point, the DOM would immediately sell one contract for a profit of +6 pips and would immediately thereafter move the remaining contract's stop to −6 pips at 1.3124. Whew! That was the sound of the trader breathing a sigh of relief. Six pips of profit have been booked and maximum loss has been moved from −24 pips on two contracts to ZERO for the entire trade. Heat has been removed; it's gone for this trade. One can easily imagine smiles all around on the occasion of this event. Remembering that an MM trader's Job One is to achieve free trades, this is one very big reason why. Preservation of emotional capital through achievement of free trades is not only Job One, it is a longevity enhancer in the life of a trader. The fact that free trades also preserve financial capital magnifies their benefits many fold.

The ability to take heat is one thing, one very important thing in the life of a trader. Letting profits run is an another equally important aspect to trading that is facilitated by the disciplined use of a preconfigured DOM. Picking up where we left off with our example scenario, the trade has achieved RR after generating considerable heat and has only one goal left to achieve—Target 2. If 1.3130 was the starting line, Target 2 at 1.3155 is the finish line, a distance of +25 pips. That distance offers the potential for substantial profit but also presents some challenges because of its length.

Waiting for +6 pips of profit to be booked is one thing, waiting for +25 pips of profit to be booked can be quite another. Whereas the waiting period for a small profit such as +6 pips can often be very short, on the order of a few seconds, the waiting period for a profit of +25 pips will almost always be longer, sometimes much, much longer. And therein lies a problem based on the temptation to book profit and run. Just as the mouse makes it exceedingly easy to move stops further away from initial settings, it is even easier to exit a position with one mouse click before its intended target has been hit. If +25 pips of profit is the goal, +15 pips might seem to be a good enough approximation, especially if the trader has taken an extended period of heat or if x-number of preceding trades were losers. Some profit, *any* profit, can seem tantalizing attractive in such cases. But whenever a trader succumbs to the temptation to cut profit short, its effect on longer-term profitability is not being given due consideration. Successful MM trading—in fact, *all* successful trading regardless of methodology—is based on cutting losses short and letting profits run. That is another trading truism that should not be forgotten.

For the MM trader, there is another overriding reason for allowing a profitable trade to play itself out to completion by waiting for Target 2 to execute. Failing to do so without a compelling technical reason violates one of the fundamental tenets of the methodology: the −23 percent target! The very foundation of MM trading stipulates that trade entries occur at or near HWB, first targets are set to execute at levels calibrated for achieving RR trades, and secondary targets are set to −23 percent or beyond. To successfully realize the full potential of MM trading, traders must strive to squeeze maximum profit out of each and every trade. That being said, as we will see later, there are occasional situations in which bailing out early before −23 percent is hit is called for, but those situations are always based on solid technical evidence. If it is clear that the market is reversing and will do so before −23 percent is hit, then accepting a somewhat smaller profit would be the prudent thing to do.

■ Running Off the Road

Scenario 2 (breakeven) and Scenario 3 (maximum loss) show hypothetical examples of the inevitable crashes that can and do occur as traders navigate the mountain range of price. Breakeven trades are like little fender benders that represent relatively trivial nuisances along the road to profitability. The other name used for breakeven trades—scratch trades—makes the fender bender analogy even more fitting. Breaking even and losing nothing more than commission cost is like getting a little scratch or ding in a trader's vehicle. Not too big a deal, not something to worry about. The vehicle is scratched but is definitely still road-worthy and ready to enter the race when another solid entry point presents itself. On the road to profitability, it's like a brief, forced pit stop.

A maximum-loss trade is something more—it's like running a trader's vehicle off the road. Its other name—full stop-out trade—indicates that a trade has sustained something much more serious than a scratch. Because the damage is more serious, the trader should take extra caution going forward. In and of itself, one full stop-out trade isn't sufficient to take a trader's vehicle out of a race. It is sufficient, however, to raise a yellow flag warning that extreme caution should be used while reentering. If after reentry a second consecutive full stop-out occurs, many experienced MM traders will take themselves out of the race for a period of time. For MM day traders that usually means stopping for the day. That second consecutive full stop-out is a red flag indicating that the trader is not reading the market correctly and should sit on the sidelines before making additional costly errors and crashing again and again. Removing oneself voluntarily before a downward spiral of full stop-out after full stop-out is allowed to develop is most often the best course of action to take in such situations.

■ When Multiple Contracts Just Aren't Possible

As mentioned earlier, multicontract trading in major trading instruments like the ES or 6E is often not possible for MM traders with small accounts. Following the 1 percent rule, the maximum loss per trade for a $10,000 account is $100, which represents only eight ES ticks or 6E pips. Trading two contracts of either would entail setting initial stops to a mere four ticks or pips, a level that is much too tight for safely trading either contract. Volatility in either one frequently moves price to plus or minus four from entry, often in the blink of an eye. Sound money management principles would prohibit setting stops so tight; there would be simply too much risk in doing so. Trading with such tight stops would virtually guarantee that full stop-outs would be the norm rather than the exception. One way around this is to trade one contract in an all-in/all-out trade. An initial eight-pip stop on one 6E contract would generate a loss of $100 before commission; an initial six-tick stop on one ES contract would generate a loss of $75 on full stop-out. Either falls within the guidelines of the 1 percent rule.

The settings for a one-contract all-in/all-out 6E trade would be:

Initial stop = −8 pips
Moved stop = 0 pips after price hits +8 pips from entry
Target = +25 (moved to Fibonacci −23 percent level after entry)

The risk-reward ratio for this trade would be 3.125:1 based on a maximum loss of $100 (8 pips × $12.50) and a maximum profit of $312.50 (25 pips × $12.50). Therefore, it meets all of the risk-reward criteria for MM trading.

The settings for a one-contract all-in/all-out ES trade would be:

Initial Stop = −6 ticks
Moved Stop = 0 pips after price hits +6 ticks from entry
Target = +25 (moved to Fibonacci −23 percent level after entry)

The risk-reward ratio for this trade would be 4.166:1 based on a maximum loss of $75 (6 ticks × $12.50) and a maximum profit of $312.50 (25 ticks × $12.50). Therefore, it meets all of the risk-reward criteria for MM trading.

But what about an account size of $5000? Trading either the full-size 6E or ES would be out of the question given the 1 percent rule. However, the situation is not hopeless for small-account traders because E-micro's have arrived on the scene to provide an alternative, at least for the EUR/USD and eight other currency pairs. Carrying a value per pip of $1.25, an eight-pip full stop-out on two contracts of the E-micro M6E would result in a loss of only $20 ($1.25 × 16)! The 1 percent rule would allow a per-trade loss of this magnitude on an account of only $2000. This benefit comes with a cost, however. Because the CME's E-micro contracts are relatively new and because Smart Money is busy trading the full-sized 6E and not the M6E, liquidity in the latter is extremely limited. As a result, initial stops should be set much wider to accommodate low levels of liquidity thereby skewing the risk-reward calculations. For these reasons, traders would be wise to paper-trade E-micro contracts in a simulated DOM to try them out first before applying real capital. As a final note, traders with a $10,000 account could also try the half-size E7 (EUR/USD) as an alternative to the 6E.

■ Why 90 Percent?

While working your way through this chapter you might have wondered about its title. Why do MM traders call the process of executing and managing a trade the "90 percent factor"? While that exact percentage might be subject to debate, the critical importance of each step in the processes detailed in this chapter is not. Placing trades at the right price based on solid technical data and managing those trades with strict discipline and rigor is 90 percent of the trader's endeavor. In MM trading, it's where the rubber meets the road.

CHAPTER 6

Three Types of Trade Setups

There are three types of trading setups that we use to trade the markets:

1. The traditional 50 percent measured move (MM).
2. The extension 50 percent MM.
3. The 61.8 percent MM.

Our goals are to know how to identify these trade setups and how to trade them. In order to confidently execute our trades, we must examine which setups to trust, and know when to watch for confirmation and participation.

■ The Traditional 50 Percent Measured Move

The traditional setup is when we pull back 50 percent or halfway back of an initial rally. Many traders that are first made aware of this pattern in the market often ask how high-frequency trading (HFT) programs trade this setup. In Figure 6.1, the market is rallying away from the lows of 1.2627, and we continue to trail the market. Every time the market touches its 50 percent MM, the HFT programs will fill new orders. In this particular example, price did not make a pullback into a full 50 percent retracement until the market came off a high of 1.3324. There was a resting limit long waiting to fill its buy order at 1.2976. The same programs that are waiting to buy the

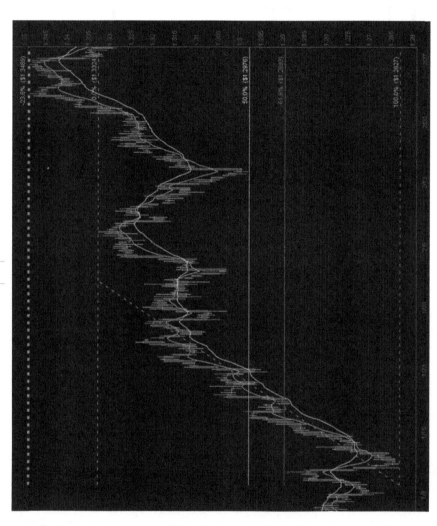

FIGURE 6.1 Traditional Measured Move Long

Source: thinkorswim®.

50 percent MM are now waiting to take profit at the markets 123 percent profit target at 1.3489. This target is 123 percent of the total distance of the initial rally that was trailed from lows to highs by the program trades. In this example, the market took 14 days and traveled 513 pips to its target. Every 50 percent MM that a program trades has its own unique profit target.

The inverse of the example in Figure 6.1 is true as well. In Figure 6.2, the market is selling off and a program is following price down as it sells off. As it is falling, its sell order is ready just in case the market happens to pop up into a 50 percent MM short. In this particular example, after coming off its lows at 1.3600, the market took three days to come back up into its 50 percent MM short. That means the programs were waiting patiently for three days for the optimal price to sell at 1.3865. As soon as the trading program's sell order was filled at 1.3865, it again waited patiently for 4 more days until the price traveled a distance of 384 pips to its profit target at 1.3481. If only it were as easy for humans to be as patient as computers. Don't worry, we can be.

A Series of Measured Moves

Now we understand how a traditional MM is structured. We now need to examine how a series is structured, and how measured moves can string together to form a series. A series of traditional MMs is when the market moves from its 50 percent entry, to its 123 percent profit target, and after hitting its profit target, pulls back into its next traditional MM. In Figure 6.3 we have a rally of off 1,195.50, where a program patiently waited for a pullback. The program was finally given an opportunity to buy a 50 percent MM at a price of 1,223.00. The pullback gave this program a 123 percent profit target of 1,267.47. Once the target was completed, a new program looked for an entry that started from the last low at 1,222.25 and continued to wait for a new pullback opportunity. The next pullback at 1,243.75 traded its 50 percent measured move, and gave a new 123 percent profit target at 1,274.31. The next setup reaches its target and the series of MMs continues indefinitely. We will talk about how and when a series can end, and what to do later in the chapter.

Which Traditional Measured Moves Not to Trust

There are some traditional MMs that we should not trust without first observing their participation. We also need to recognize when a possible series of measured moves could fail. There are very specific clues to look for that can give you a heads-up on a questionable MM. Also a larger time frame's profit target could break the last MM in a series. In Figure 6.4, a series of smaller

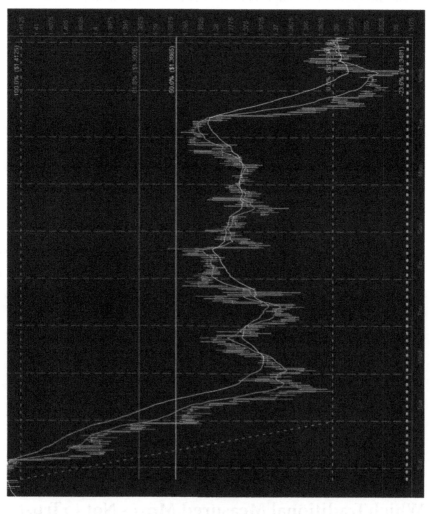

FIGURE 6.2 Traditional Measured Move Short

Source: thinkorswim®.

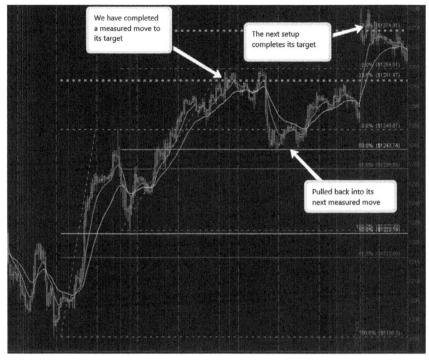

FIGURE 6.3 Series of Traditional Measured Moves

Source: thinkorswim®.

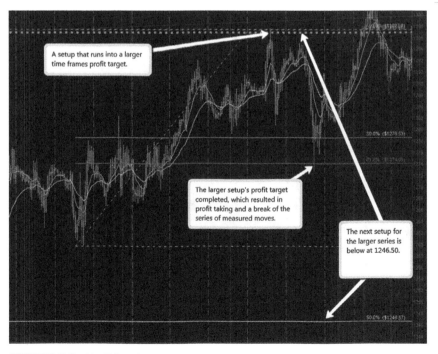

FIGURE 6.4 Traditionals Not to Trust

Source: thinkorswim®.

traditional MMs runs into a larger time frame's 123 percent profit target at 1,297.00. After the larger measured move profit target was completed, profit taking resulted in the break of the smaller series of MMs at 1,278.53. This is a sequence of events that can be very predictable and foreseen beforehand. The next MM in the larger time frame's series is down below at 1,246.57. An analogy that we like to use in this situation is "we are too close to the trees to see the forest." We will talk about this in the next chapter.

■ The Extension 50 Percent Measured Move

The extension 50 percent MM is formed when we rally past the profit target of a traditional MM. Extensions can be longs or shorts, but in the following example we will be talking about an extension long MM. Normally, in a traditional 50 percent MM, the market will hit its 123 percent profit target and make a pullback into its next traditional 50 percent. In Figure 6.5 we have an example of a market that has hit its 123 percent profit target at 1,296.59, but did not pull back. When the programs that are waiting for the next traditional MM observe the market making new highs, they stop looking for a traditional MM. They begin a new extension 50 percent and start trailing price from the top of the last retracement. In Figure 6.5, the extension

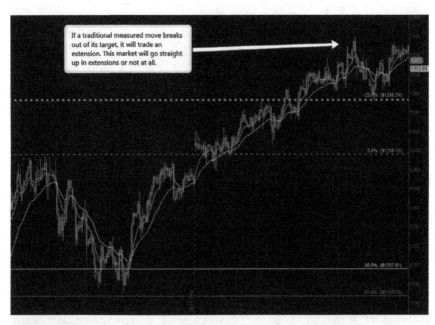

FIGURE 6.5 Traditional Measured Moves Become Extensions
Source: thinkorswim®.

begins from the previous highs of the 1,268.13. The program patiently waits for price to pull back into its new extension at a price of 1,296.59. The program's buy order is filled, and then it patiently waits for price to travel to its 123 percent profit target. Technical analysts will recognize this pattern in the market. They will recognize them as bull and bear flags, and they would be absolutely right. These specific patterns are how bull and bear flags develop. The MM gives us a specific price and profit target for patterns in the market.

The Extension 50 Percent in a Series

A series of extensions can be in longs or shorts, but in this example we will be talking about a series of extension shorts. In Figure 6.6 a series of extensions from an anchor of 2,498 start when we have completed and gone through a 123 percent profit target at 1.2442. The program uses the lows of the previously completed extension at 1.2498 again, and continues to wait for a retracement into the first new 50 percent MM. The lows of 2,425 gave the market its pop back into the next extension 50 percent MM at 2,461. The program's 2,461 extension 50 percent short entry gives a 123 percent profit target of 2,408.

In Figure 6.7, we examine the continuation of the series of extension 50 percent MMs, which uses the same anchor of 1.2498.

In Figure 6.7, the second extension in this series is drawn from the same anchor of 2,498. The programs continue to trail price down and patiently wait for the market to rally back up into its 50 percent extension again. This time the market sold a 2,427, which gave a new 123 percent profit target of 1.2325. The next setups will continue to use the same anchor of 2,498 for each subsequent new extension. Extensions 50 percent MMs, just like traditional 50 percent MMs, can also continue indefinitely.

Which Extensions Not to Trust

As you'll remember, extensions begin when a series of traditional 50 percent MMs goes through its 123 percent profit target. The very first extension cannot be trusted with a limit order, and needs only to be observed. In Figure 6.8, a traditional 50 percent MM from 1.2375 hits and goes through its 123 percent profit target at 2504. We know that if price goes through a

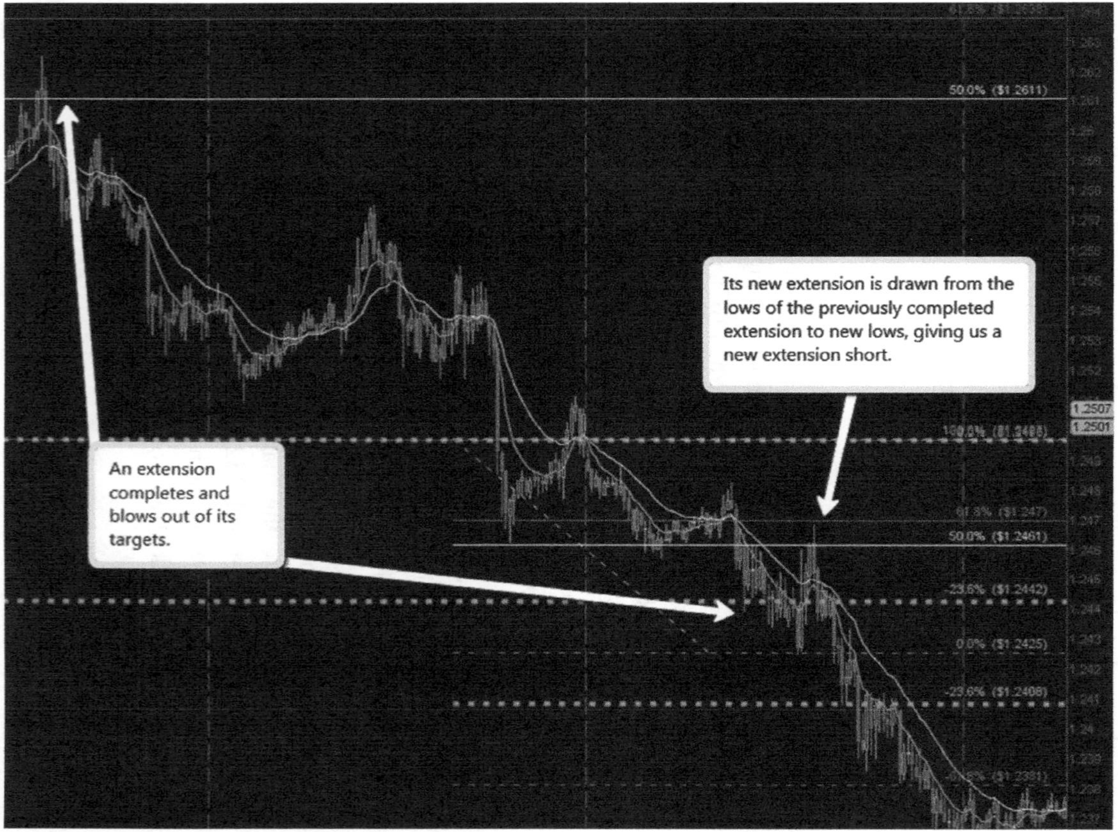
50.0% ($1.2611)
Its new extension is drawn from the lows of the previously completed extension to new lows, giving us a new extension short.
1.2507
1.2501
An extension completes and blows out of its targets.
50.0% ($1.2461)
-23.6% ($1.2442)
0.0% ($1.2425)
-23.6% ($1.2408)

FIGURE 6.6 Extension Short
Source: thinkorswim®.

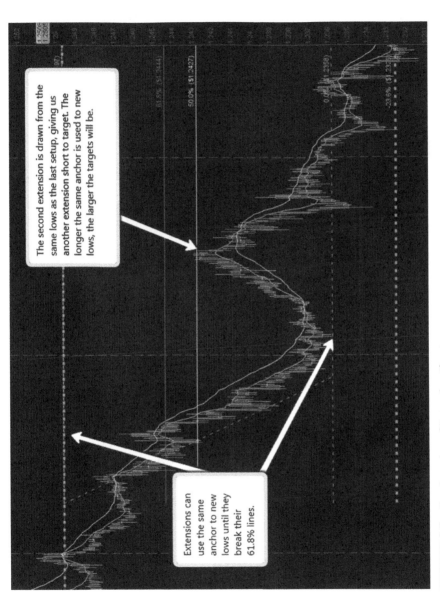

The second extension is drawn from the same lows as the last setup, giving us another extension short to target. The longer the same anchor is used to new lows, the larger the targets will be.

Extensions can use the same anchor to new lows until they break their 61.8% lines.

FIGURE 6.7 Continuation of Extension Shorts

Source: thinkorswim®.

THREE TYPES OF TRADE SETUPS

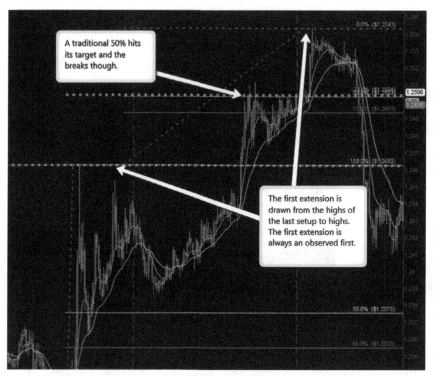

A traditional 50% hits its target and the breaks though.

The first extension is drawn from the highs of the last setup to highs. The first extension is always an observed first.

FIGURE 6.8   Extension Failure
Source: thinkorswim®.

traditional 50 percent MM's target we start a new extension. The new extension is drawn from the highs of the last traditional at 2,483, and continues to draw new highs until price pulls back into the extensions support level at 2,504. In the example in Figure 6.8, we see that the first extension fails. This reinforces the need to observe the very first extension after price goes through a 123 percent profit target. Once the first extension is witnessed, the rest of the extensions from that anchor are safe to trade to their profit targets.

■ The 61.8 Percent Failure

The 61.8 percent failure is less of a trade setup and more of a signal that the current series of MMs, whatever that series might be, is over. Failures can be longs or shorts, but in this particular example we will be talking about a series of MM longs that have failed. In Figure 6.9, a traditional MM

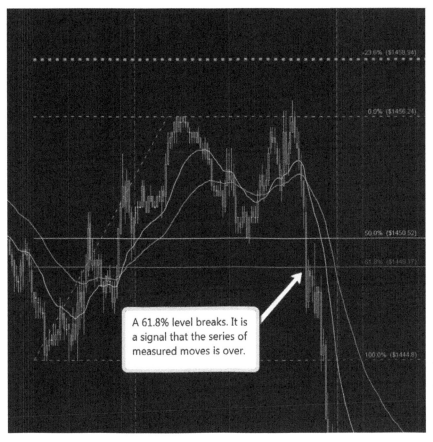

FIGURE 6.9 Failed Longs
Source: thinkorswim®.

long at 1,450.52 was bought at its 50 percent and then had an expected 123 percent profit target at 1,458.94.

Price failed to break out of its previous highs and immediately came back into the original entry. Failing the second test of the MM long at 1,450.52 and piercing the 61.8 percent level breaks the series of MM longs this market was trending in. This is one of the most important patterns in the market to recognize. It is the end of one trend and the beginning of another. In this example, the next short setup would be the next MM.

The 61.8 percent failure can signal a new trend, or assist us into a larger trend. In Figure 6.10, a traditional 50 percent MM is trading and has a 123 percent target above.

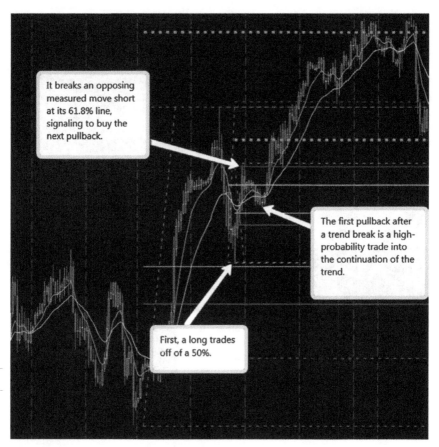

It breaks an opposing measured move short at its 61.8% line, signaling to buy the next pullback.

The first pullback after a trend break is a high-probability trade into the continuation of the trend.

First, a long trades off of a 50%.

FIGURE 6.10   First Pullback after a Trend Break
Source: thinkorswim®.

An opposing traditional 50 percent MM short is broken, signaling an opportunity to buy the next pullback in the continuation of the larger trend. The first pullback after a trend break is a very successful trading opportunity, and is many times the beginning of a brand new trend. The 61.8 percent failure can be disappointing and exciting at the same time. It can be disappointing if you are in a trade and are waiting for a trend break as a profit target. Everyone wants the trade they are in to last forever. It can be exciting because it represents a brand new trend, and the beginning of a new trend is the best time to enter. One must remember that being kicked out of a trend that has been profitable is a success. It is also an opportunity to get on the ground floor of a brand new trend. One door shuts, another one opens.

What 61.8 Percent Failures Not to Trust

We learned that the 61.8 percent failure can signal a new trend or help us into a larger trend. There are certain times that this is a dangerous trade. There are very specific clues to look for that can give you a heads up on a questionable MM. If a 61.8 percent failure turns into a retest of previous highs or lows, do not trust the next MM. In Figure 6.11, a traditional 50 percent MM is bought at 1,301.64. An opposing MM fails at 1,311.26, giving us an entry into the larger trend. Normally, immediately after a 61.8 percent failure, the market will pull back and give its entry. In this particular example, it instead runs up and retests its previous high. The pullback after this previous high has traded is a dangerous trade, as sellers will participate in what many technical analysts would call a *double top*. It will more than likely retest its previous support or resistance before continuing in its trend. This idiosyncrasy of the market is extremely powerful to recognize, as it can be avoided and profited from.

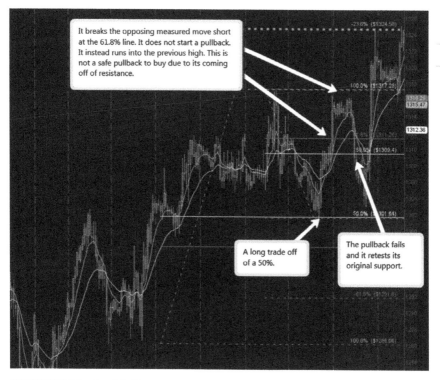

It breaks the opposing measured move short at the 61.8% line. It does not start a pullback. It instead runs into the previous high. This is not a safe pullback to buy due to its coming off of resistance.

A long trade off of a 50%.

The pullback fails and it retests its original support.

FIGURE 6.11 Double Top
Source: thinkorswim®.

■ Why Is This Important to Your Trading?

The three types of measured moves are the traditional, the extension, and the 61.8 percent failure. The computers that trade these MMs have rules they follow in the progression of a trend. They all have a cause and effect when they work together and a very specific order in which they trade in. The market travels in traditionals, then to extensions, and then straight up. If we ever fail the 61.8 percent level, the trend changes. Knowing this order gives us a sequence to trade in. In the next chapter, we will learn about the three different time frames the markets move in.

For more information, watch the video titled "The Three Types of Fibonacci Trade Setups," available at http://eminiaddict.com/?p=5439.

CHAPTER 7

Using Multiple Time Frames to Trade

The strategies in this chapter will give us the tools to identify the path of least resistance. We will be exploring concepts that will allow a trader to identify trends and future prices of any market. We will review how to execute these opportunities when they arise and how to manage our trades once we are in them. Here, we open a road map that will allow us to predict future profit targets days, months, and years ahead of time.

■ Time Frames and Russian Dolls

In the previous chapter, we looked at four measured moves (MMs) in the real world and at how they evolved over time. What we didn't dwell on was the precise time frame particular to each chart; instead, we focused on the contours of motion exhibited in each. Before moving on to further investigation of the MM methodology, we need to lay some basic groundwork for considerations of time. Without an informed perspective on the multiple time frames over which market prices move, a trader's success will prove elusive at best.

Traders the world over use a wide variety of time frames as they trade the markets. Position traders typically use yearly, monthly, and weekly charts. Many

Swing traders step it down a notch and use primarily monthly, weekly, and daily charts as their time horizons are often shorter than those utilized by position traders. Day traders tend to use charts of the shortest time increments—one-hour and 15-minute charts are very common among this group. But beyond the 15-minute time frame, for day traders the preferred charts of even shorter duration show the greatest variety. Not only are day traders' short-term charts based on time, they can also be based on a specified number of trades taken or the range in which previous trades occurred. These last two types of charts are not time-based at all. One is central to the MM methodology.

To recap, MM day trading primarily uses three types of charts: daily, 15-minute, and tick. In MM-speak, the first two are named for their time values: daily and 15-minute. The last of the three is called micro because it is the shortest in duration. So we have three characters in the play of market movement in day-by-day MM trading: daily, 15-minute, and micro. Enter the Russian dolls.

Even though you might not have known that what you were looking at was a matryoshka or a babushka, you might have seen what is commonly called a Russian nesting doll. First created in 1890, a Russian nesting doll is a set of painted wooden dolls of decreasing size in which the entire set can be contained within the largest one. The tiniest one goes inside the next-smallest one, which goes inside the next-smallest one, and on and on until the largest doll contains all the rest. In MM trading, Fibonacci-based MMs on micro, 15-minute, and daily levels often nest in much the same way with micro MMs inside of 15-minute MMs inside of a daily MM. Of course, being fluid and in motion continuously, the nesting in MMs isn't fixed and final the way it is in Russian dolls, but the metaphor still applies and is useful for purposes of visualizing market forces.

■ The Path of Least Resistance

If you aren't familiar with Alexander Elder, he is a trader and author of the book *Come Into My Trading Room* (John Wiley & Sons, 2002). With the majority of his concepts revolving around lagging indicators, he has introduced an important concept. The problem with traditional lagging indicators is that they tell you only what has already happened. Lagging indicators are based on moving averages; thus, they give completely different buy and sell signals on different time frames. The weekly chart could be in a sell signal, while the rest of the signals are in a buy signal. Dr. Elder focused on lining up indicators on multiple time frames to get a clearer picture of the path of least resistance. He realized that if the weekly, daily, 4-hour, 1-hour, and 15-minute charts were all pointing the same direction, then he had found the path of least resistance. This is a concept we want to implement in our trading, but instead of basing the path of least resistance on lagging moving average–based indicators, we will be basing it on price.

■ Trading the Trend

There is a saying, "I know just enough to be dangerous." This couldn't be further from the truth in regards to trading. Many traders, after gaining some knowledge about the markets, will find that they have a very good understanding of the way the market moves. It will often lead to having dangerous opinions about the market and its future direction. Traders can often find themselves picking tops and bottoms. You will often hear the terms *overbought* and *oversold*. These terms come from a need to explain the lagging indicators that so many traders still use. An example would be having an indicator in a buy signal for two weeks, while the market is still making new lows. This is a nice way of saying that this market can't go any lower, or this market can't go any higher. Trust me—it can and it will. There is no such thing as overbought, oversold, expensive, or cheap. Markets that are making lows can continue to make new lows. Markets that are making new highs can continue to make new highs. Markets that are expensive can and will get more expensive. Markets that are cheap can and will get cheaper.

Why Do Markets Continue to Make New Highs?

Markets continue to rally because they are fueled by sellers at highs. Markets will stop making new highs when the very last of the bears turn bullish right at the highs. Without sellers at highs, the market has no fuel to push through to new highs. This is where we get the saying, "The market climbs a wall of worry."

Why Do Markets Continue to Make New Lows?

Markets continue to sell off because they are fueled by buyers at lows. Markets stop making new lows when the very last of the bulls turn bearish right at the lows. Without buyers at lows, the market has no fuel to push through to new lows.

A New Concept

Trade the trend until it fails. Picking tops and bottoms is unprofitable and unnecessary. You do not need to predict the major turns in the market to be successful. The programs that trade our markets do not pick tops or bottoms, either. Their algorithms and trading rules are based on cause and effect. The only real benefits from picking the top or bottom of a trend are bragging rights and ego, neither of which add to our bottom line. A beginner trader feels that he or she has to identify the top or bottom of the market, while an experienced trader knows he doesn't have to. A beginner trader always feels as if he or she has missed the move, while the experienced trader knows that the market will show a change in the trend and give an entry into it.

■ What Time Frame Should We Look At?

You will often hear a trader who uses an indicator-based strategy asking this question. They reason is that moving average–based indicators will give different buy and sell signals on different time frames, and will never give you a specific price to enter or exit the market. Indicator-based strategies will have a different signal on every time frame. When trading price, there is no such thing as the wrong time frame. The trade setups on the weekly chart will be the same on the daily and the 4-hour chart. The trade set-ups that setup on the 15-minute chart will be the same on the 1-hour and 30-minute charts. Price will always be the same across all time frames. Different time frames will have different setups inside of them, but price will be the same. The difference is that some setups will be visible, and some will not. One fact traders have to remember when trading price is this: the largest time frame is the most powerful, and the smallest time frame is the least powerful.

It is important to remember the rules for MMs include:

- The biggest trend wins.

- Trade the trend until it breaks.

- If the trend breaks, a new trend will begin.

- Respect the weekly trends the most and the micros the least.

Types of Multiple Time Frames

We should clarify and define the multiple time frames that we will be referring to in the rest of this chapter. For simplicity, when talking about the weekly trend, we are referring to the largest trend that we can see zoomed all the way out with 10 to 20 years of data. It is only when we can see the big picture that we can see the largest trends that the market has to offer. The weekly chart is the most powerful trend. It has the highest odds of completing its target, and all of the other time frames are at the will of this larger trend.

The Weekly Trend Figure 7.1 is a monthly chart of the Standard & Poor's (S&P) 500 in a traditional 50 percent MM short. In a downtrend, as the market is selling off, we start our draw from the top of our range and trail it to the lows. We wait for the market to retrace back up into its traditional MM short. Once this 50 percent is touched, it gives us a 123 percent target toward which to trade. This sized time frame is the most powerful in our markets. It took three months to set up in its entry,

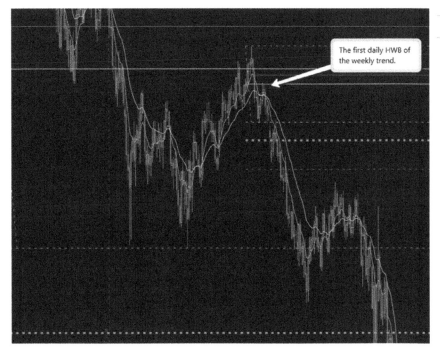

The first daily HWB of the weekly trend.

FIGURE 7.1   Weekly Traditional Measured Move Short
Source: thinkorswim®.

and it took another three months to complete to its target. Some traders may speculate that they don't trade that large of a time frame, so why should they care? The answer is that this type of market direction and prediction model gives us clues to trade the path of least resistance. It tells us the general direction we should be trading. As we drill down into the smaller time frames, we have opportunities to trade this extremely large trend to its target.

Typically, the only reason a trader isn't trading this large a time frame is that he or she doesn't know it exists. As with many disciplines in life, opportunities are invisible to the unprepared. The weekly time frame is the largest time frame and takes the longest to complete. Typically, these are long-term swing trades, and they give the market its most powerful direction. The weekly charts are the path of least resistance, and all of the other trends will be either with or against them. The smaller time frames will always be easier to trade in the direction of this trend. We have the ability to enter into the weekly trend by drilling down and looking at the daily trend entry opportunities. As the larger weekly trend reacts to its resistance level, the market sells off hard, falling away from its traditional 50 percent short MM. This first reactionary trade is where most retail traders would chase the sell-off for fear that they had missed an entry into the sell-off. The professional traders know from experience that the market will give them another entry. The retail trader chasing the sell-off produces a rally as they are squeezed out of their positions into the next traditional 50 percent MM short. The next daily 50 percent MM short is drawn from the all-time highs to the low. We then wait for price to come back to our 50 percent retracement to sell. The daily MMs will give us an entry into the weekly target.

The Daily Measured Moves   We consider the daily trend the second most powerful trend. It has very high odds of completing its target. All of the other time frames are at the will of this daily trend, except the weekly trend. Figure 7.2 is a daily chart of the S&P 500 in a traditional 50 percent MM long. It took six weeks to set up in its entry, and it took another six weeks to complete to its target. This type of long-term target gives us a direction to trade the market. The daily trend can be traded with 15-minute MMs. The daily trend takes anywhere from 10 days to 3 months to complete its target. The first 15-minute MM is the best entry into the larger daily trends target. By now, you are starting to see a pattern developing. If you see a larger trend

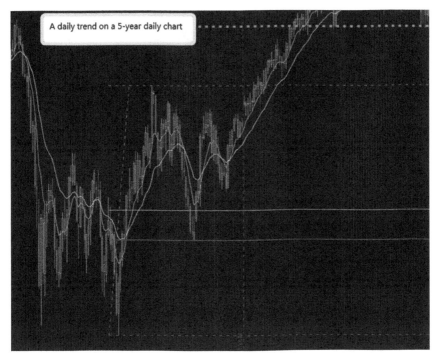

A daily trend on a 5-year daily chart

FIGURE 7.2   Daily Traditional Measured Move Long
Source: thinkorswim®.

developing, you can go to the next smaller time frame to look for an entry into the trend. Sometimes there are not any entries into the daily trend. A new event or an after-hours test can ensure this. Whatever the case may be, don't chase the market. The 15-minute chart will give us entries into the daily MMs.

The 15-Minute Trend   We refer to this medium-term time frame as the 15-minute trend, but it can be anywhere from 5 minutes to an hour long. The only requirement is that we see the details inside the daily MM trend. The 15-minute trend takes anywhere from 5 minutes to 10 days to complete its target. The time frames where we can see the inner workings of the larger trend will be where we spend the most time trading. There can be anywhere from 2 to 12 trade setups per day depending of the time of the year. The key to the smaller time frames is to remember the larger weekly and daily trend's path of least resistance, and trade the 15-minute MMs in that direction. It is a great way to filter opportunities during the

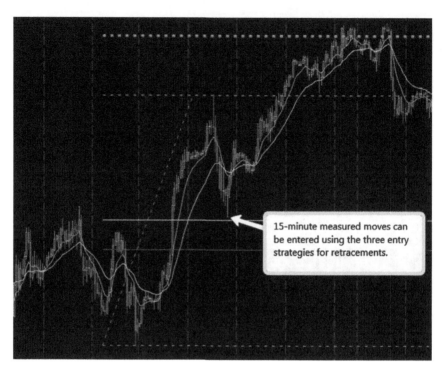

15-minute measured moves can be entered using the three entry strategies for retracements.

FIGURE 7.3 15-Minute Measured Move Long
Source: thinkorswim®.

day. Sometimes there will be situations where you miss your entry's getting filled, or you might not trust the support or resistance level setting up as a safe opportunity. Whatever the case, don't chase the market (see Figure 7.3).

The Micro Trend We generally consider the micro MMs the weakest trend, but they are incredibly powerful. Think of the micros as a tool to enter the larger trends. The micros are at the will of all the larger time frames, so it is very important to know your surroundings. The micro MM is the best entry into the 15-minute trends target. A micro trend will complete its target within 1 to 30 minutes, and there can be hundreds of micros that make up the structure of the larger time frames (see Figure 7.4). The first micro after a trend break is the best micro to trade. The farther a market gets away from the beginning of its larger trend, the less reliable the micros become. There is a way to drill down farther to help time the entries of the micros, as well using the tick and tick hooks. We will cover those in later chapters.

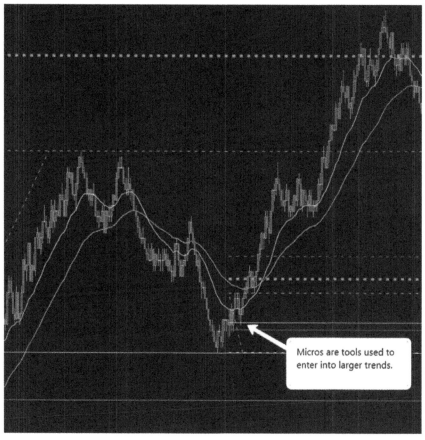

Micros are tools used to enter into larger trends.

FIGURE 7.4 Micro Measured Move Long
Source: thinkorswim®.

■ Why Is This Important to Your Trading?

I'm sure that you have heard the saying, "Cut your losers short, and let your winners run." Drilling down from large time frames to the smallest lets us fine-tune our entries. You will find that once you know where you are in a trend, you will find it much easier to hold your trades to their targets with confidence. You might be at the beginning of a weekly long, off a pullback of a daily MM, entering a trade on the 15-minute trend, and realize your entry has a 250-point target! Many traders don't have a target for a trade once they are in it. Traders have many inventive ways to enter a trade, but very few to identify the exit. When a trader knows their target, they can understand their risk-reward ratio. Once you know your risk-reward ratio, you gain a positive expectation for a given opportunity. Any trader who has had a problem with pulling the trigger entering a trade probably didn't know the target. Once you can justify your reward, it's easier to make a case for an entry.

For more information, watch the video titled "The Three Timeframes to Trade," available at http://eminiaddict.com/?p=5580.

CHAPTER 8

Three Entry Strategies for Retracements

We have identified the types of trade setups and the different time frames to trade our futures and foreign exchange markets. Now we need to talk about the techniques that we can use to enter into the trade.

■ The Goal

Our goal for this chapter is to define how to identify the three types of entries. The object of having an entry strategy is to develop a rule-based system that will allow the trader to enter into the market in a consistent way. Consistent rules produce consistent results. By the end of the chapter, you will know what to do with these opportunities and how to enter them.

Front Runs and First Targets

The front runs and first targets are different for every market. These are the normal front runs and first targets that work the best for their respective markets (see Figure 8.1).

FIGURE 8.1 Front Runs

Insturment	/ES	/YM	/TF	/NQ	/6A	/6B	/6C	/6E	/6J	/GC	/ZB
Initial Stop Loss	−6 ticks	−12 ticks	−12 ticks	−12 ticks	−12 pips	−12 pips	−12 pips	−12 pips	−12 pips	−12 ticks	−8 ticks
Front Run	+2 ticks	+4 ticks	+4 ticks	+4 ticks	+4 pips	+4 pips	+4 pips	+4 pips	+4 pips	+4 ticks	+4 ticks
First Target	+2 ticks	+6 ticks	+6 ticks	+6 ticks	+6 pips	+6 pips	+6 pips	+6 pips	+6 pips	+6 ticks	+4 ticks
Adjusted Stop Loss	−4 ticks	−6 ticks	−6 ticks	−6 ticks	−6 pips	−6 pips	−6 pips	−6 pips	−6 pips	−6 ticks	−4 ticks

■ The Three Entry Strategies

As you learned in the previous chapter, the daily time frames have entry opportunities on the 15-minute chart. The 15-minute time frame has entry opportunities on a micro chart. The trends that you can identify on the larger time frame have entry opportunities on the next smallest time frame down. There are three different entry strategies that you have the opportunity to use. These opportunities happen in the same order every time, for every measured move (MM).

The First Test

The first test, or entry strategy, is the highest-probability trade and will always have the most volume behind it. A first test has the best participation and has the highest probability of hitting a first target. The reason the first test is best is that programs that have already identified the trend will be waiting with their limit orders to be filled at a specific price, right in front of an MM. There will always be competition at the first test, which is why the 50 percent MM has to be front run in order for a limit order to be filled.

Figure 8.2 shows a traditional MM on the E-mini S&P 500 Index (ES) futures market that has pulled back into its first test entry. When a market

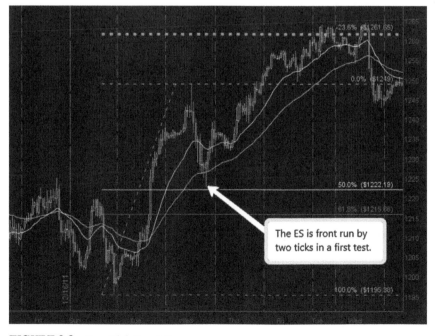

The ES is front run by
two ticks in a first test.

FIGURE 8.2   Two-Tick Front Run
Source: thinkorswim®.

is trading a series of MMs, the trader places his or her limit order and waits for price to pullback in the first test entry. The sooner the order is placed the better, as the orders are filled in the order they were placed. Placing limit orders is a first-come, first-served situation. As you see in Figure 8.2, the ES is front run by two ticks. The two-tick front run is the front run that has worked on the ES futures for the past six years. It would not be uncommon in a very aggressive rally or sell-off to see a front run of three ticks. The normal stop for the ES futures is six ticks. That means that if the market dipped more than six ticks into the original entry, the trader would be stopped out for a small loss. The first target on the ES futures market is +2. After the first target is hit, the stop is automatically moved from −6 to −4, resulting in a reduced-risk (RR) trade.

How to Trade a First Test   There are three very important rules to follow when trading a first test:

1. If you are not filled in the first test you must immediately *pull your limit order*. Sometimes the market will be in an extremely aggressive uptrend or downtrend. The first tests in these situations can be front run by extremely large distances. If the market does not fill your limit order, sellers have chased the first test. This makes the retest of the first test dangerous, as the first participants have the potential of causing a stop run. This phenomenon is the reason that the second test is the most dangerous test. There is an old saying in the futures markets: "Fade the first test, and go with the second." Basically, trade the first test, and don't trade the second, it could break out.
2. *Never chase an entry.* Wait for the next opportunity to enter the market with a second test entry. Chasing a trade setup is not a planned trade, and when a trade isn't planned, bad things can happen.
3. If you are ever taken out of a first test trade at breakeven, *stop.* Prepare for the next entry opportunities, the *front Run of the second test,* or wait for the *trend break and next MM.*

The Front Run of the Second Test

The next entry opportunity is the front run of the second test. This is by far the riskiest entry, but it also has the best risk-reward ratio. You now know the unspoken rule of futures markets that says, "Fade the first test, and go with the second." It is for this reason that we consider the second test the dangerous test. The second test entry is best used with a smaller size and with a smaller stop. This entry can be used if the first test was missed or when you were not ready with a limit order in a first test. It can also be used if you didn't trust or were apprehensive of the first test for some reason like a news event of an opposing MM. You can front run the price that traded in the first test with a stop right below the low in a long or right above the high in a short.

It is very important to mention again that the second test in the futures and foreign exchange markets are usually the most dangerous test. That being said, instead of being RR trades, they should be all-in/all-out trades with smaller size. It is always better to trade a second test entry than to chase a first test if your order was not filled in a first test (see Figure 8.3).

How to Trade the Front Run of the Second Test   Figure 8.3 shows a traditional MM long that has pulled back into its entry. If for some reason you were not able to trade the first test, you must wait for the second test entry. It is very important that a trader use limit orders, as the entries are very price specific. The sooner the limit order is placed the better, as orders are filled in a first-come, first-served situation. The pullback in Figure 8.3 is a MM long; the previous low on the ES is front run by two ticks with a limit

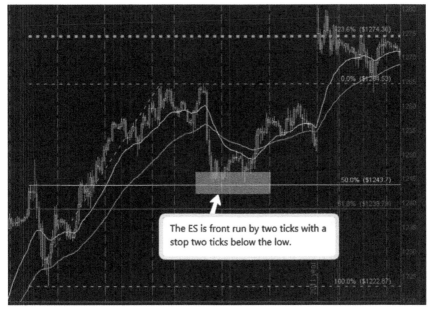

FIGURE 8.3   Front Run of the Second Test
Source: thinkorswim®.

order. The stop is placed two ticks below the participation level for a total of a four-tick stop. The exact opposite would be true of this situation if we were in a series of MM shorts.

There are three rules that are important to follow when trading second tests. These rules will help you enter the market consistently and keep you safe.

1. If your limit order is not filled and price moves away, *pull your limit order*. Sometimes the market will be in an extremely aggressive uptrend or downtrend, but that does not give us permission to chase the market with a market order.
2. *Never chase an entry*. Wait for the next opportunity to enter the market with a trend break entry and a next MM.
3. If you are ever stopped out of a trade, prepare for the next entry opportunity.

The Trend Break and Next Measured Move

The last opportunity for entry is the trend break and next MM. This entry can be used if the first test was missed. It can also be used if you didn't get filled in a front run of the second test, or for some reason you didn't trust the second test. Figure 8.4 shows a trend break of an opposing MM. We call this a confirmation of a support or resistance level. The pullback in Figure 8.4 has traded its first test and successfully moved away from its entry. It has also given a second test entry that was front run and moved away, giving the trade room away from its entry. Breaking the opposing MM tells us two things:

1. It confirms the trend and a new pullback into that trend.
2. It confirms the profit target. (In this example, the target is 1,274.36.)

This will begin a new series of MM longs moving away from the new long setup into the profit target.

How to Trade the Trend Break Figure 8.4 shows the trend break of the opposing MM. Figure 8.5 shows the next MM after the trend break. The next MM on the ES futures is front run by two ticks and uses its normal reduced risk trading strategy. As a rule of thumb, the next MM can be traded with the same specifications as a first test, which is shown in Figure 8.1. The next MM is an excellent entry into the larger trends target. It also has an excellent risk-reward ratio as the entry and stop are relatively small.

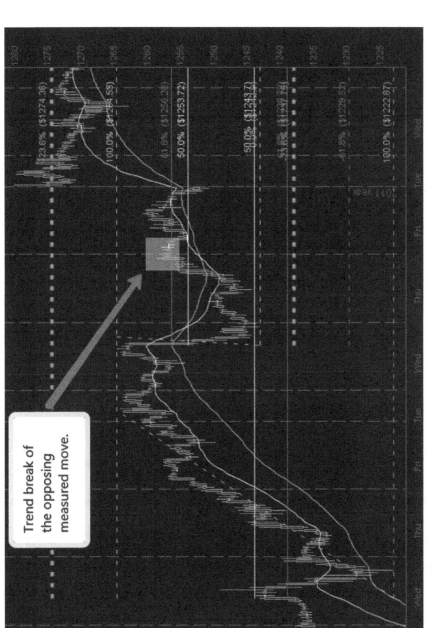

Trend break of
the opposing
measured move.

FIGURE 8.4 Trend Break

Source: thinkorswim®.

THREE ENTRY STRATEGIES FOR RETRACEMENTS

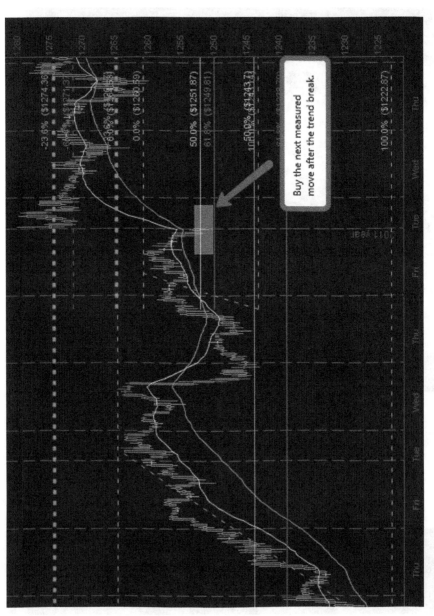

FIGURE 8.5 Measured Move after Trend Break

Source: thinkorswim®.

There are three rules that are important to follow when trading next MMs. These rules will help you enter the market consistently and keep you safe:

1. If your limit order is not filled and price moves away, *pull your limit order.* Sometimes the market will be in an extremely aggressive uptrend or downtrend, but that does not give us permission to chase the market with a market order.
2. *Never chase an entry.* Wait for the next opportunity to enter the market.
3. If you are ever stopped out of a next MM, *stop.* The market is sloppy or the trend has not clearly been defined.

■ The Progression of Entries

We have specific rules for each entry technique, but it is important that we put them together as a progression of patterns in the market that occur very frequently. The progression of entries has rules to follow as well:

1. The first test will always be the best. Program trades will fight over the right to get filled. If you do not get filled, wait for the second test.
2. The second test has a higher risk entry into the trend. Second tests should use tighter stops and reduced size. If you do not get filled, wait for the trend break and next MM.
3. The opposing MM break confirms the target. It gives you permission to place a limit order and buy the next MM. If you do not get filled in the next MM, you will have to wait for the next setup to start all over again.

■ Why Is This Important to Your Trading?

In order to have consistent results in our markets we must have consistent order entry techniques. The markets have certain times of the day and night that have a high participation and volume. We will talk about those times in the next chapter. Sometimes the market will give us setups that we might not trust in their first test because of the conflicts with time of day or news announcements. We also might have times in which setups in the second test will be against larger opposing MMs. These strategies give us a systematic way to participate in those trends in the safest way possible. The biggest dangers in our markets are in many ways self-inflicted. The danger exists when trades are chased instead of planned. There is a trader's saying that says, "You never get smarter once you are in the trade." Traders are at their best when they are planning the next opportunity.

In essence, our job as traders involves being able to:

- Recognize the trend.

- Identify the setup.

- Get filled.

- Not second-guess it.

- Hold the trade to its target.

For more information, watch the video titled "The Three Types of Entry Strategies for 50% Retracements," available at http://eminiaddict .com/?p=5500.

CHAPTER 9

The Seasonality of Markets and the Best Times to Trade

M any traders find measured moves in the market and become extremely excited, and rightly so. They tend to jump right into the market at the very first opportunity that they see, but there's more to it than that. There are safe times in the market to trade and dangerous times in the market to trade. Certain times of the year, month, and day are found to have a higher expectation of successful trades. The goal of this chapter is to help you identify the best months of the year, days of the week, and hours of the day to trade. It will help you plan your entries during the New York Stock Exchange (NYSE) and European market hours. It is important to know when to employ trading techniques that you have learned.

■ The Big Picture

Historically, the best months to trade give us our big picture for the market. The monthly, weekly, and daily setups give a clear direction and target for long-term investments. In bull markets, price patterns repeat year after

The Months

● January	Bull	Fast
● February	Bull	Fast
● March	Bull	Fast
● April	Best Month to Sell	Fast
● May	Worst Month to Buy	Med
● June	Consolidation	Slow
● July	Consolidation	Slow
● August	Worst Month to Sell	Med
● September	Best Month to Buy	Fast
● October	Bull	Fast
● November	Bull	Fast
● December	Bull	Fast

FIGURE 9.1   The Best and Worst Months to Buy and Sell

year, decade after decade. There are generally, in trading terms, two different seasons of the year to trade. Those two seasons are called *risk on* and *protect profits*. It is important to remember that most funds in the market are long-only funds. What this means is that they don't short the market. The best months to trade are also associated with the fast and slow times of the year (see Figure 9.1).

The Months

You might have heard the old saying "sell in May and go away." Others might have heard the term "Santa Claus rally." There is more truth to these sayings about the stock market than you might think. Over the years, patterns have developed and observations have been made based on performance, participation, and the speed of price action in the market. The best time to be bullish in the market has been from Labor Day through Memorial Day. More specifically, observations have been made that tell us April is the best month to sell, and May is the worst month to buy. The end of August is the worst month to sell and the best to be a buyer. Historically speaking, for long-term bullish positions, one should focus on being a buyer in late August and September, and on taking profits in late April and early May.

Studying the Past

Markets repeat themselves year after year and decade after decade. What has worked in the past can be observed and profited from in the future. You have heard the saying that you should trade a trend until it fails. Seasonal markets can be traded just like trends. They continue to trade the same way year after year until the trend fails. We can't predict the future until we understand what has happened in the past. Let's look at an example of seasonal markets in our past. Figure 9.2 is a chart of the S&P 500 over the course of three years. In bull markets of the past 100 years this pattern is witnessed every spring and fall.

It is no coincidence that the best months to sell are at the beginning of the summer, and the best times to buy are at the end of the summer. From the end of May to the end of August you will experience one of the slowest trading and participation periods witnessed in the markets. The 90 days of summer represent some of the most dangerous markets that traders will encounter. They are full of consolidations on the daily charts, tight intraday trading ranges, and low participation breakouts and breakdowns.

◼ A Money Manager's Year

Based on what we know about money flow during the year coming in and going out of market, we can make some assumptions about what the typical broker or money manager's year would look like. It wouldn't revolve around Christmas or New Year's like a typical American's would. It would revolve around the summer, and more than likely, around their children's summer vacations. If you have ever been in New York City during the summer, you'll notice that the streets are empty, the subways are desolate, and there are few people roaming the streets in the morning. Money managers are at their summer homes in the Hamptons enjoying time with their families (see Figure 9.2).

Summer

A money manager's summer would begin a little something like this: Coming into Memorial Day, they would more than likely be fully invested with their new client money from the previous August–September. The first course of action would be to analyze their portfolio risk. They would do two things: take partial profit, and completely hedge their exposure to the market. Once they are hedged for the summer, they would be free to enjoy their summer vacation with their families. They leave their support staff to take care of the daily operations. New client money is still coming in. Sounds nice, doesn't it? This explains why we have such low volume during the summertime. The Big Money has prepared itself for a choppy, low-participation summer.

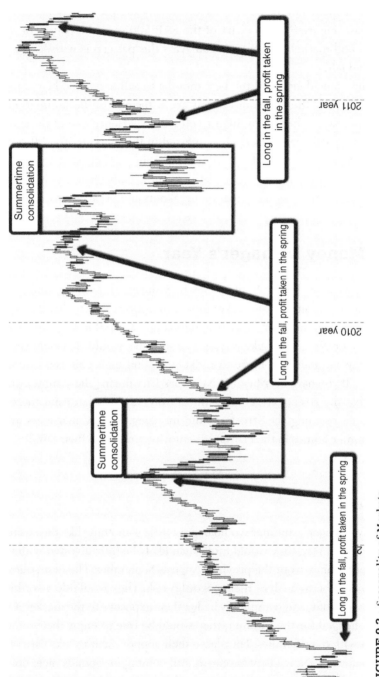

FIGURE 9.2 Seasonality of Markets

Source: thinkorswim®.

Fall

After a long Labor Day weekend, most people start coming back from summer vacation. It is no coincidence that historically market volume picks up at this time of the year. The first course of action at the beginning of the fall would be to take all of the protection trade "hedges" that had created the "risk off" trade of the summer. This unwinding of summertime hedges is why most traders associate the end of the summer with increased volatility. The next course of action would be to put all of the new client money to work that accumulated over the summer. This is the real beginning of the year for money managers. This is the time of the year that the "risk on" trade goes on. It is the historical accumulation of positions going into the winter and what some call the "Santa Claus rally." This is what makes August the worst month to sell the market and September the best time to buy.

Winter and Spring

Historically, the period from October to March has the best returns on investment over the past 100 years. This is the continuation of the accumulation of positions. The cycle is about to repeat itself. As we come into the months of April and May, the market starts to slow down. Volume starts to dry up and the participation with the trend starts to falter. The beginning of the summer is upon us again, and the cycle repeats. This is what historically makes April the best month to sell or take profit and May the worst month to be a buyer going into the consolidation of the summer. From a long-term investment perspective, being a bull from September to March and going on a long summer vacation begins to look very appealing.

■ The Days

There are certain days of the week that are better for intraday traders. Mondays and Fridays are notoriously the worst days of the week to be a trader. A normal, average white-collar American workweek isn't so different from a top Wall Street executive's. Let's examine why.

Mondays are slow; it's the first day back from the weekend. Everyone is dragging their feet into work. Traders are digesting the news from the weekend and their portfolio risk. We can easily imagine the top money managers all sitting around big tables designing their game plans for the week. This is why volume on Monday morning is so lethargic and low volume. Smart

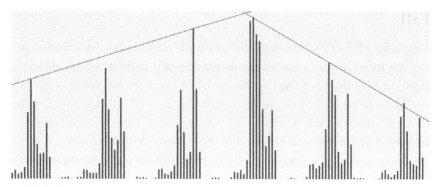

FIGURE 9.3 Weekly Volume Curve
Source: thinkorswim®.

Money is planning. Volume on Mondays usually starts to pick up in the afternoon around 1:30 to 2:00 P.M. It is pretty easy to connect the dots here. By the time everyone is finished with their morning meetings, it's lunch time. That is why volume increases on Monday afternoons. The biggest risk on Mondays is letting the market trick you into thinking that nothing is going on or that it is an untradeable market. Every Monday is the same, and the faster you realize it, the easier they are to deal with. As an intraday trader, it is beneficial to trade Mondays with half-size positions if at all.

In Figure 9.3 you can see that Mondays and Fridays are the lowest-volume days. Tuesday through Thursday are the highest-volume days. There is also something we call participation. Participation is when traders are actively accumulating positions. This higher participation is what makes the market more technical in the middle of the week. Tuesdays, Wednesdays, and Thursdays are normal trading days. Volume comes in, participation is high, and the market trades quickly. The setups that exist during this time in the markets are where all the heavy lifting for the week comes from. Any big accumulation or the hedging of positions comes from this time in the markets. The middle of the week is when most trades will set up and complete their targets.

Friday afternoons are one of the most dangerous times for a trader. By the European session close at 11:30 A.M. Eastern Time on Friday most of the volume has dried up. Traders have taken profit for the week by either closing positions or hedging their gains over the weekend. Price action can become extremely slow and at times seem to stop trading. By the European ,session close, all trading is done for the day. All of the money managers are making a dash for the exits to enjoy the weekend. As a trader, it is incredibly important to recognize the drop-off in participation. It is more profitable to not trade Friday afternoons than to get caught up in the slow price action at the end of the week.

■ The Hours (Best and Worst Times to Trade)

Just as there are good and bad days of the week, there are good and bad times of the day to trade. There are notable times during the day and night that have recurring patterns. The trading week begins during the hours from Monday night into Tuesday morning. To make things easier, all times are quoted in Eastern Time.

Figure 9.4 shows the market opens and closes for all the major time zones of the world. Some of these time zones overlap and can create better times to trade.

2 A.M. ET: The Frankfurt German Stock exchange opens. This begins the trading day and breaks the slow, choppy price action of the Asian session. You will want to make a habit of observing the direction for the first 15 minutes of the day.

3 A.M. ET: The London stock exchange opens. This is when real volume comes into the market. The 3 A.M. time frame is often the exact reversal of the German market open. Normal volume occurs from the European open to the beginning of Europe's lunch break.

5:30 A.M. ET: The beginning of Europe's daily doldrums, and the slowest part of the day. We usually witness profit taking in the opposite direction from whatever the main direction of 3:00 A.M. ET was. This is Europe's lunchtime reversal period and the beginning of a consolidation.

7:30 A.M. ET: The end of Europe's daily doldrums. This is frequently a stop run from the consolidation of the slow, choppy lunchtime trade.

8:00–8:30 A.M. ET: The NYSE futures open. This is when the volume from the United States overlaps the volume of Europe. From 8:00 A.M. to

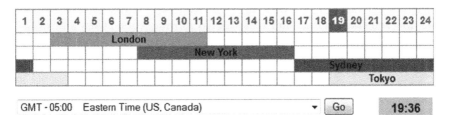

FIGURE 9.4 Best and Worst Times to Trade

11:00 A.M. the highest volume of the day is produced. Most traders don't realize that this is the best time to trade futures and foreign exchange markets. An attempt into the gap fill for the open occurs 90 minutes before the opening bell.

10 A.M. ET: There is a trading rule most stock traders live by, and it is based purely on experience. The first 30 minutes of the trading day is a no-trade zone. That means no moving stops, closing positions, or modifying orders. Most Big Money will wait for the first half-hour after the bell to place the first trades of the day. What this creates is a volume push at the 10 A.M. time frame that is extremely reliable. The 10:00 A.M. time frame produces more entries than any other, and is often the high or the low of any given trading day. The volume and participation from the 10:00 A.M. time frame lasts for 90 minutes.

1:30–2:00 P.M. ET: The end of the daily doldrums. Just like the end of the Europeans' lunch, this is many times a stop run of the consolidation from the slow, choppy lunchtime trade. The afternoon is usually a continuation of the trend that began at 10:00 A.M.

3:30–3:45 P.M. ET: The last volume push of the day. This is an attempt to get the market back to its average price of the day. This target is calculated by adding the high of the day plus the low of the day, divided by the current price trading.

Based on past experience, trades that originate during these times have a high expectation for hitting their profit targets and being successful trades.

■ The Worst Times to Trade

It is extremely important to know when it is safe to make a trade that has volume and participation behind it. Knowing when *not* to trade is even more important. You know from the preceding information that the summer can be slow and choppy. You know that Monday mornings and Friday afternoons have lower expectation for profitable trades. There are also times during the 24-hour trading day that are dangerous to trade.

6:30 P.M.–2:00 A.M. ET: The beginning of the Asian session. The Asian session is known as the daily doldrums of the 24-hour trading day. To help put this time of the day into perspective, think of Europe being fast asleep and New York just getting ready for bed. Two continents with the majority of the world's trading volume are asleep. It is best to stay out of markets altogether.

5:30 A.M.–7:30 A.M. ET: Europe's daily doldrums, otherwise known as Europe's lunch break. Trades should always be limited to the larger time frames or managing positions that are already on.

9:30 A.M.–10:00 A.M. ET: The NYSE opens at 9:30 A.M. The first half-hour of the day is a no-trade zone. This is one of the most volatile times of the day. It is filled with reactionary trades and stop runs. Over time, it has been found that trades initiated between 9:30 and 10:00 A.M. have a very low expectation of being profitable. Wait for 10:00 A.M. like all the other professionals, and you will be much more profitable and happy as a trader.

11:30 A.M. ET: The 11:30 reversal period, the beginning of the daily doldrums, the European session close. We usually witness profit taking and a reversal from the main direction of the 10:00 A.M. time frame. This is the beginning of the lunchtime trade for the United States and the slowest part of the day. Most traders take profit and make plans to go to lunch.

■ The Typical Money Manager

Based on observations in the market, the life and schedule of a hedge fund manager or money manager starts to take shape. Based on the volume and participation, it seems as though they work nine months out of the year. It looks as though they take the whole summer off someplace sunny and warm. During those nine months they are not on vacation, they come to work on Monday morning and don't really get any work done until Monday afternoon, or even Tuesday morning. Meanwhile, at the end of the week on Friday they finish up by lunch and leave for the weekend. The three days they do get work done, they are active from 10:00 A.M. to 11:30 A.M. and then take a two-hour lunch. They come back at 1:30 P.M. for a late afternoon push into the close until 4:00 P.M. That sounds like a pretty great schedule.

■ Why Is This Important to Your Trading?

As longer-term trend traders, knowing the seasonal bullish and consolidation times of the year helps us plan for future trends and targets. It puts us on the right side of the market, going with the flow instead of against it.

Knowing the seasonality of the larger time frames puts us in a position of power for long-term investment gains.

As intraday trend traders, it is important to know when these forces are at work in the market. We can't move the market with our volume and size. We have to grab hold of the coattails of larger, more powerful programs and traders, and hitch a ride to our profit targets. Knowing the specific days of the week that have the highest participation helps us focus on trading positions that stick. We must always match the speed of the market that is trading. Most new traders associate slow trading markets with safety and fast markets with danger, when exactly the opposite is true. Fast markets should be traded quickly and will produce more trades than slow markets. Slow markets should be traded slowly and will naturally produce fewer trades.

Now that you are aware of these periods in the markets, put them to the test.

For more information, watch the video titled "Seasonality," available at http://eminiaddict.com/?p=5700.

CHAPTER 10

Tools for the NYSE

There are many market indicators that have been developed over the years to help traders navigate the markets. In this chapter, we will identify the difference between leading and lagging indicators. We will go over how to use our tools to enter very precise trades with positive expectations during the New York Stock Exchange (NYSE) trading session. We will also learn how to use the tools together to paint a clear picture of the path of least resistance.

■ Lagging versus Leading Indicators

The difference between a lagging and a leading indicator is that a lagging indicator is telling you what has already happened. Leading indicators tell us what is going to happen, and at what price it will happen. Almost all indicators are based one way or another on moving averages. These moving averages have cleverly been packaged in different ways over the years and sold to traders and investors. Moving averages tell traders what has already happened, and leads them into chasing the market. The goal is to use only the tools (leading indicators) which help us predict future price movement and targets before they happen.

■ Tools for the NYSE

The leading indicators discussed in this chapter include:

■ Bank

■ Breadth

■ The tick

■ Tick hook

■ Time and sales

■ The trend

Bank

"Bank" is a nickname used for the Nasdaq banking index. It is an index of 417 securities that are smaller local banks, bank corporations, and financial institutions throughout the United States. Our stock market indices are heavily weighted with financial institutions. The direction of the Nasdaq banking index can give us clues to the direction of the market. Being that Bank is an index, it is not traded. This allows Bank to give a clear picture into the smaller financials being bought or sold during the day. Figure 10.1 shows a historical sector weighting of the Standard & Poor's (S&P) 500 from 1990 to 2012. You will notice that the financials have the second-highest weighting of the S&P 500, second only to the tech sector. Over the years, Bank has shown an uncanny ability to give intraday direction clues even if the indices are going the opposite direction. Bank will give you clues to trust or not trust a rally. It will also give you clues when to trust or not trust a sell-off.

How to Use Bank   There are specific rules to follow to get the most out of the Nasdaq banking index. The rules are as follows:

1. In uptrending markets, if Bank is making new highs all by itself and the indices are not, Bank can and will eventually drag the indices higher. Always trust Bank.
2. Sometimes the indices will rally without Bank. If the indices are making new highs and Bank is not following, do not trust the rally of the indices. What you are witnessing is a potential bull trap. Always trust Bank.

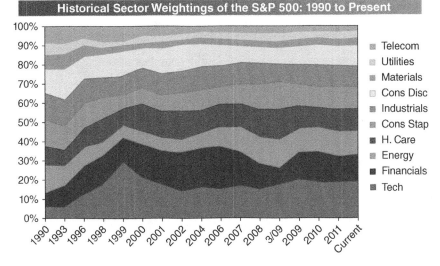

FIGURE 10.1 Historical Sector Weighting

3. In downtrending markets, if Bank is making new lows all by itself and the indices are not, Bank can and will eventually drag the indices lower. Always trust Bank.
4. Sometimes the indices will sell off without Bank. If the indices are making new lows and Bank is not following, do not trust the sell-off of the indices. What you are witnessing is a potential bear trap. Always trust Bank.
5. Don't fight Bank.

Breadth

Market breadth is the ratio of up volume versus down volume, to advancers versus decliners of their respective markets. Both the NYSE and the Nasdaq have separate market breadth readings.

The up volume is the amount of trading volume that is buying or pushing the market higher. The down volume is the amount of trading volume that is selling or pushing the market lower. The ratio tells us who is winning the fight, in numerical form. In Figure 10.2, the relative ratio of up volume versus down volume is –1.2:1. This tells us that the sellers are winning.

The advancers are the amount of instruments that are being bought or being pushed higher on the exchange. The decliners are the amount of instruments that are being sold or pushed lower on the exchange. The ratio of the two tells us who is winning the fight in a numerical form. In Figure 10.2, the relative

NYSE	SYMBOL	LAST	Relative	Percent		NASDAQ	SYMBOL	LAST	Relative	Percent
	$UVOL	1,387,003		43.8%			$UVOL/Q	609,826		45.0%
			-1.2 :1						-1.1 :1	
	$DVOL	1,718,660		54.3%			$DVOL/Q	695,162		51.3%
	$TVOL	3,167,653					$TVOL/Q	1,356,338		
	$ADVN	2,296		56.0%			$ADVN/Q	1,439		59.0%
	Diff (A-D)	491	1.3 :1				Diff (A-D)	437	1.4 :1	
	$DECN	1,805		44.0%			$DECN/Q	1,002		41.0%
	$TRIN	1.580	$TICK	258			$TRIN/Q	1.640		
	DJX	13,103	-22	-0.17%			COMPX	3,077	4.0	0.13%
	SPY 500	1,414	-1.4	-0.10%			VIX	16.49	0	0.85%
	RUT 2000	814	3.88	0.48%						
	IRX	1.00	0.05	5.00%			TLT	125.84	0.30	0.24%
	TNX	16.30	-0.19	-1.17%						
	Yield Cur	15.30	-0.24	-0.23			USD Index	81.38	0.00	0.00%

FIGURE 10.2   Market Breadth Display

ratio of advancers versus decliners is 1.3:1. This tells us that there are more up-ticking versus down-ticking instruments, and that the buyers are winning.

How can the sellers be winning while the market has more advancers then decliners? Great question.

How to Use Breadth   There is a very important rule to follow when using and following breadth. Many new traders find this tool but fail to use it properly. They run into a situation where there are conflicting messages and fail to recognize the clues the market is showing them. They end up throwing this incredibly powerful tool away without truly understanding it. The breadth rule says *you must always know where the breadth ratios started for the day at the opening bell.*

Positive breadth means an upward-trending market, and negative breadth means a downward-trending market. It is important to know where market breadth starts; otherwise, we will not know where it is going. For example, you walk into the trading day without seeing where the breadth opened and are witnessing a negative breath reading of –10:1. The market, at first glance, is considered to be weak, and you might initially be inclined to sell a resistance level. What if the opening breadth reading was –50:1, and over the course of the day had made up all the ground from a –50 to a –10? The market would have to be very strong to make up that kind of ground. Although the breadth reading would still be negative, the Breadth Rule would help us to see that the market is actually strengthening. Opening market breadth helps us confirm the direction for the day.

The Tick

The NYSE tick is used as a tool to help us enter into the market. It measures very brief overbought and oversold moments in the market. An easy way to think of the tick is to compare it to a respirator machine. The NYSE tick represents the inhale and exhale of the market. The "tick" is the NYSE up/down ratio, and it represents the number of stocks that are ticking up, less the number of stocks that are ticking down on the NYSE. The time frame we look at on the tick chart is extremely important, as we want to look at the smallest inhale and exhale that we can see. The best time frame to view the NYSE tick is the 1-minute chart. This is an extremely fast time frame and, without a filter, can give us false signals. The best filter for the tick is a one-period simple moving average.

Figure 10.3 is an example of a tick chart in the top and bottom of its range. A +400 reading is a brief overbought moment, and a –400 reading is a brief oversold moment. The +400 overbought tick reading is an excellent time to sell when we are in a series of measured move (MM) shorts and down trending. A –400 oversold tick reading is an excellent time to buy when we are in a series of MM longs and uptrending.

Tick Hooks

A tick hook is when a brief overbought moment (a high tick) is turning into a brief oversold moment (low tick). The opposite is also true; a brief oversold moment (low tick) is turning into a brief overbought moment (high tick). A tick hook's purpose is to help us enter a trade with the highest probability of success. Tick hooks also help us time free and reduced-risk (RR) trades. Selling briefly overbought moments gives us the highest probability of getting an RR trade in a short. Buying briefly oversold moments gives us the highest probability of getting an RR trade in a long.

Figure 10.4 is an example of high ticks and tick hooks that correspond with a traditional MM short. Every time the tick moves above +400 on the tick chart, price is sold at our traditional MM short. This high tick gives us a signal to enter the traditional MM short. This high tick has a very high probability of becoming a successful trade that quickly moves away from its initial entry. As you can see in Figure 10.4, there are multiple entry opportunities into the traditional MM. This entry technique works in MM longs and shorts, as well as normal support and resistance levels.

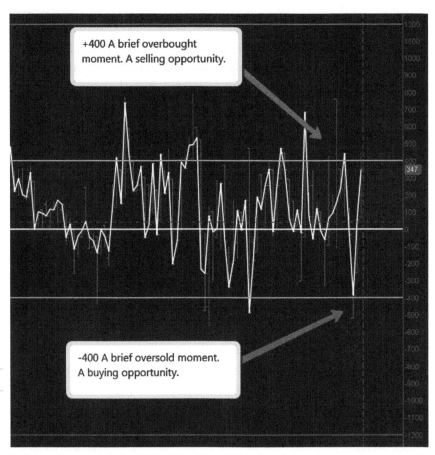

FIGURE 10.3 Tick Chart
Source: thinkorswim®.

Time and Sales

Time and sales are the receipt tape of the market. The "tape" tells us the transactions that are taking place in real time. We use the tape to help us see participation at keys levels in and around MMs. We trade very specific prices, and the tape gives us clues during the day to the amount of contracts being bought and sold at MMs. The reason it is important to watch the tape, is that if we are in long setups on a given day, we see heavy participation from only buyers. We want to be able to identify where the participation is and trade only in the direction of those specific MMs.

How to Trade Time and Sales Figure 10.5 shows a traditional MM short that is trading its entry. In this situation, you witness large blocks of

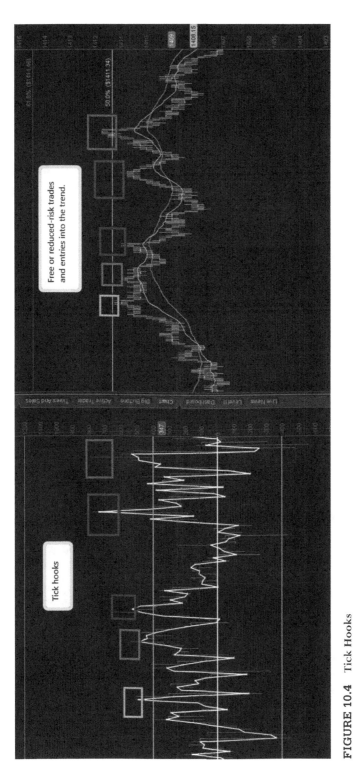

FIGURE 10.4 Tick Hooks
Source: thinkorswim®.

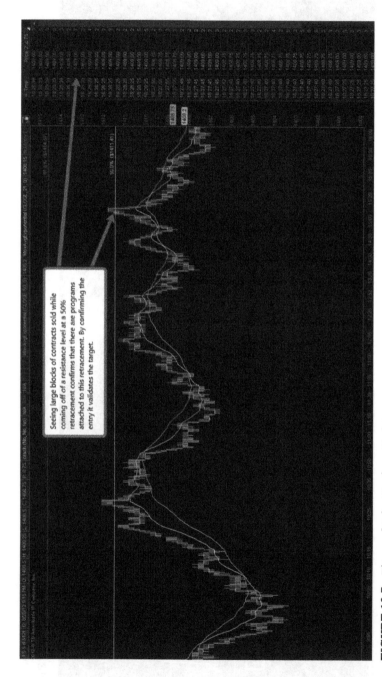

Seeing large blocks of contracts sold while coming off of a resistance level at a 50% retracement confirms that there are programs attached to this retracement. By confirming the entry it validates the target.

FIGURE 10.5 Time and Sales Confirms Resistance

Source: thinkorswim®.

contracts being sold as price moves down. Witnessing large blocks of contracts sold at an MM short confirms that there are programs attached to the trade setup. By confirming the entry has participation, we also validate its target. The programs that are selling into the MM have a specific price set for their profit target.

Trade the Trend

The last and most powerful tool for the NYSE trading session is the trend. The daily trend and target will always be the default direction of the market and the path of least resistance. Our other tools confirm or oppose the trend that is in play. The market will not always move directly to the target of the daily trends. These tools will help you understand the day as it develops and whether or not you have a day that is trading in the direction of the daily trend and the path of least resistance, or against it.

■ Using All the Tools Together

Using all the tools together is like watching an artist paint a portrait. At first, you have only clues to what the artist might be painting. As time goes on and more clues are acquired, a clear picture comes into view. The more validating tools we have, the more reliable and trending the market will be. Think of the tools that have been talked about in this chapter as pieces of evidence in a trial. Any one piece of evidence by itself might not be enough to make a case to a jury. All of the clues together give a glaring bullish or bearish case to the jurors. It is extremely helpful to think of this analogy while you are trading, and ask the question, "If I had to make a case to a jury whether this market was bullish or bearish, what would my evidence be?" By making the case to the imaginary jury you are taking an emotional step back, and make a logical, rational argument. As you get more accustomed to analyzing these tools, you will be able to make strong cases for or against the major trend of the market. These tools will also help you make crucial decisions when MMs make themselves available. They will also give you confidence to see those trades to their profit targets. To review, the largest trend of daily MMs gives us the road map. Bank and breadth reinforce our bias for the day. The smaller series of MMs gives us our intraday trades and targets, and the tick and tape help us into our entries.

Opportunity is invisible to the unprepared.

■ Why Is This Important to Your Trading?

Understanding these tools and how they affect the market will prepare a trader for making proactive trades. Practice and preparation will take a trader from using gut or intuition to using fact-based rules to determine the trend of the day. To review, the largest trend of daily MMs gives us the road map. Bank and breadth reinforce our bias for the day. The smaller series of MMs gives us our intraday trades and targets, and the tick and tape help us into our entries. The goal is to let the market develop and tell us what it is going to do based on the evidence it provides. These tools help us understand the path of least resistance and help us go with the flow of the market. As you familiarize yourself with these tools, you will be able to see opportunities that would not have presented themselves otherwise. Being prepared is the prerequisite to spotting opportunity.

For more information, watch the video titled "Tools of the Trade," available at http://eminiaddict.com/?p=5784.

CHAPTER 11

Tick Extremes and Divergences

In the previous chapter we identified the most powerful tools available to us during the times the New York Stock Exchange (NYSE) is open. These tools used together with the measured move (MM) give us a directional bias and path of least resistance for the day. One tool in particular deserves a chapter all on its own: the tick divergence. The tick divergence strategy is based on an observation that was made during the 2008 financial crash. The observation is relatively simple but extremely powerful. When the market is trending in an extreme way, up or down, the tick divergence tells us when it will end or if the move will continue.

■ The Types of Tick Extremes

Our goal is to identify the difference between the types of tick extremes. We will also discuss how to trade traditional high or low ticks of the day for intraday profits.

The Old Way

Traditionally, when traders witnessed the new high or low tick of the day, it was seen as a profit-taking signal and a reversal.

What changed? In the 2008 crash, we witnessed and developed a strategy around an observation in the market. It's known as the tick divergence.

The New Way

There are two different types of tick extremes:

1. The tick extreme that is the high tick or low tick of the day that matches price, but breaks trend (traditional/reversal).
2. The tick extreme that is the high tick or low tick of the day but continues its trend (divergence).

Ticks That Signal a Reversal

What is considered a traditional tick extreme for the day? A high tick of the day that matches the highs in price but breaks trend and fails to make new highs. What is considered a low tick for the day? A low tick of the day that matches the lows in price but breaks trend and fails to make new lows.

In Figure 11.1, the NYSE tick makes a new high for the day at the same time that price makes a high for the day. This is the type of traditional profit taking and reversal signal that traders are used to seeing. When price and the high or low tick of the day match, a trader can trust that the market has made a reversal and the market will change trend for the day. A safe way to trade these reversals is to confirm them with a trend break. A series of MMs will lead the market into its tick extreme. After a break of that series, a trader can trade the reversal and participate in the new trend.

■ Tick Divergences

What is a tick divergence? A divergence is when a new high or low tick is made on both the tick and on price at the same time. A tick divergence begins when the market continues to make new highs or lows in price.

What does a tick divergence signal? It signals the end of the traditional profit-taking signal and the continuation of the trend.

How long does the divergence last? It will last until the next time the tick and price make highs or lows together.

There are two types of divergences: bullish divergences and bearish divergences. Bullish divergences will make a high in price that matches the highs of the day. If the market continues to make new highs without a new high tick of the day a bullish divergence will begin. The bullish divergence will continue until a new high price and a new high tick match again. A bearish divergence is just the opposite of a bullish divergence. Bearish divergences

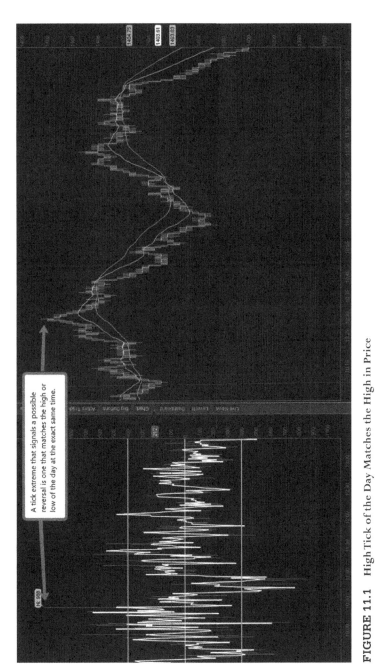

FIGURE 11.1 High Tick of the Day Matches the High in Price
Source: thinkorswim®.

will make a low in price that matches the lows of the day. If the market continues to make new lows without a new low tick of the day a bearish divergence will begin. The bearish divergence will continue until a new low price and a new low tick match again. Another way to think about divergences is that the extreme tick in the extreme price of the day matching equals profit taking. This is a signal for computer algorithms to take profit. What ends this profit-taking signal for computer algorithms is the market making another high or, in the case of a bearish divergence, a low price of the day.

Figure 11.2 shows the high tick of the day that matches a high in price. Moments later, the market makes new highs starting a bullish divergence. The bullish divergence is active and will continue to make new highs in price for the day until the next high tick of the day.

How to Use a Divergence

There are a couple of rules to guide you in using a divergence. First, if you are long and witness a bullish divergence, stay long until the next new high tick of the day. Second, if you are short and witness a bearish divergence, stay short until the next new low tick of the day. If a divergence ends, it is a profit-taking opportunity. It is only a reversal if the trend breaks and confirms. Divergences are powerful in that they allow you to stay in an intraday swing trade with confidence. All we're doing is making observations about the consistency of these events. By developing our own rules to trade these events we are taking advantage of the power behind these computer algorithms. We are in so many ways grabbing the coattails of the computer algorithms.

What Happens if the Trend Breaks?

There is both a safe way and a dangerous way to trade these events. The dangerous way is to try to pick the top or bottom in the market every time there's a new high or low tick. The only way to take advantage of a reversal safely is to wait for the opposing series of MMs to fail. If the trend breaks, wait for the opposing series of MMs to fail. If you witness a high tick that matches a high price of the day, wait for a series of longs to fail before selling short. If you witness a low tick that matches the low price of the day, wait for a series of shorts to fail before going long.

Figure 11.3 gives us an example of a high tick that matches the high of the day in price. A divergence is possible if the trend in play continues to make new highs for the day. In Figure 11.3, the high tick of the day caused

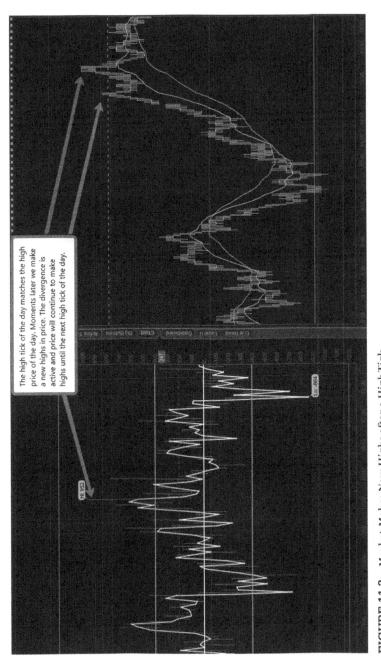

The high tick of the day matches the high price of the day. Moments later we make a new highs in price. The divergence is active and price will continue to make highs until the next high tick of the day.

FIGURE 11.2 Market Makes New Highs after a High Tick

Source: thinkorswim®.

TICK EXTREMES AND DIVERGENCES

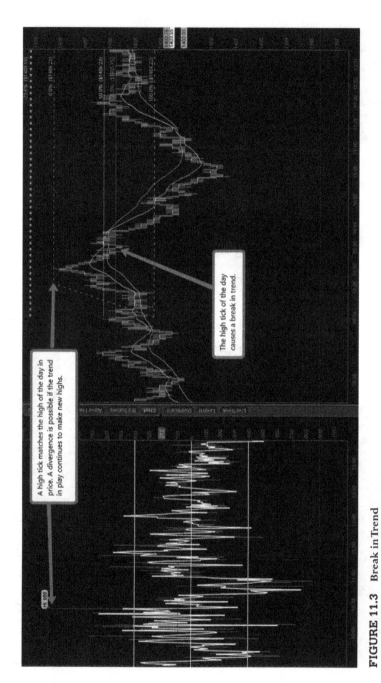

A high tick matches the high of the day in price. A divergence is possible if the trend in play continues to make new highs.

The high tick of the day causes a break in trend.

FIGURE 11.3 Break in Trend

Source: thinkorswim®.

a break in trend. The divergence over in the market has broken its series of MM longs. The high tick of the day along with a broken series of MM longs signals the high of the day. The trader now has an opportunity to participate in a new trend, the reversal from the highs of the day.

Figure 11.4 is a continuation of Figure 11.3. We witnessed the high tick of the day that matched the high price of the day. The next MM long failed, which ended the potential divergence. A high is in for the day, and we have the opportunity to sell the next MM short to enter the new trend down. The very first entry after a trend break combined with a high tick of the day that matches the high of the day is one of our very best setups. It is these setups that give us the highest risk reward ratio along with the highest participation.

Figure 11.5 is another example of the end of a divergence. The low tick of the day matched the low of the day in price. New low ticks for the day can temporarily end a divergence. The divergence is possible again if the trend in play continues to make new lows in price. In Figure 11.5, the low tick of the day causes a break in trend of the micro shorts. This break of micro shorts combined with a low tick of the day signals the lows are in for the day and a trend reversal is possible. The trader now has the opportunity to participate in a new trend, a reversal from lows of the day.

Figure 11.6 is a continuation of Figure 11.5 The low tick of the day that matched to low price of the day. The market breaking its micro MM shorts gives us the opportunity the buy the new next MM long. The very first entry after a trend break combined with a low tick of the day that matches the low price of the day is one of our very best setups. It is these setups that give us the highest risk-reward ratio along with the highest participation.

■ Why Is This Important to Your Trading?

The opportunities for profit also exist if divergences fail. If a divergence ends, it is a profit-taking opportunity. It is only a reversal if the trend breaks and confirms. The first opposing MM is the best place for an entry in a reversal. Trade the new series of MMs until the next extreme tick or until the trend breaks.

These strategies allow you to do two things with amazing accuracy.

1. On an extremely bullish or bearish trend day, the divergence will keep you in a trade to maximize your profit in the continuation of a trend.

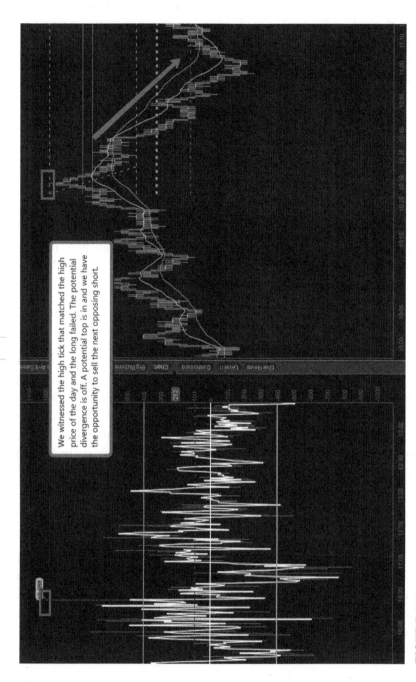

We witnessed the high tick that matched the high price of the day and the long failed. The potential divergence is off. A potential top is in and we have the opportunity to sell the next opposing short.

FIGURE 11.4 First Measured Move after a Divergence Ended

Source: thinkorswim®.

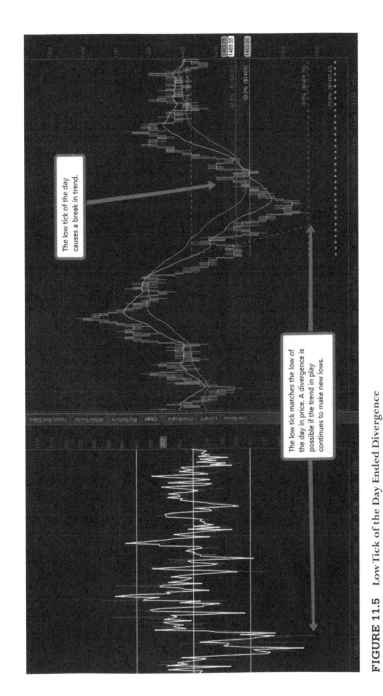

FIGURE 11.5 Low Tick of the Day Ended Divergence

Source: thinkorswim®.

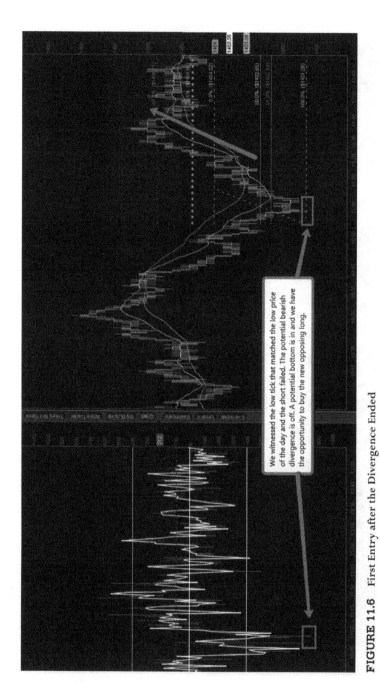

We witnessed the low tick that matched the low price of the day and the short failed. The potential bearish divergence is off. A potential bottom is in and we have the opportunity to buy the new opposing long.

FIGURE 11.6 First Entry after the Divergence Ended

Source: thinkorswim®.

2. They will also help you identify a trend reversal, which helps you end a trade as soon as the trend is over.

As traders, we're taught never to pick tops or pick bottoms, as it is dangerous and risky to do so. These are the signals that exist during the day to identify those tops and bottoms safely. Taking this newfound knowledge into the markets is extremely powerful and will serve you well for your entire trading career.

For more information, watch the video titled "Tick Extremes & Divergences," available at http://eminiaddict.com/?p=5818.

CHAPTER 12

Profiting from Gap Fills

This chapter will provide you with everything you need to know about trading a gap fill. There are three types of gap fills. We will review how to trade them, the rules to follow when trading, and which gap fills to trust and not to trust. You will learn about no-trade zones and tips that will help you profit from gap fills for the rest of your trading careers.

■ What Is a Gap?

A gap is created when the market closes after a day of trading and then reopens at a different price. The futures markets trade almost 24 hours a day during the trading week. The after-hours trading will create a gap in the morning the next trading day. The gap is the distance between where the market closed and where it opens the next day. A gap is only considered to be filled if it reaches the previous day's close during trading hours.

In What Instruments Do Gap Fills Exist?

A gap can exist in any market including stocks, futures, and forex. The markets that have the most consistent gap fills are in the futures markets. The futures contracts that have the most consistent gap fills are connected to the main indexes. They are the E-mini S&P 500 Index (ES), the E-mini Dow Jones Index (YM), the E-mini Russell 2000 Index (TF) and the E-mini

Nasdaq 100 Index (NQ). Of all the futures contracts to trade, the ES has the most consistent price action. It is also the contract that we have the most statistical information on, pertaining to the frequency of gap fills.

■ The Types of Gap Fill Scenarios

The *premarket entry gap fill,* also known as the less-than-10-point gap fill, is the standard way the market fills its gap in the morning.

The *premarket runaway gap-and-go* is also known as the greater-than-10-point gap. This is when the market gaps up and opens more than 10 points above its cash close at the opening bell. This is called the *professional gap-and-go.*

When working with gap fills, the goals would be:

■ Always have an opportunity to profit from gap fills.

■ Learn the systematic rule-based entry techniques for the New York Stock Exchange (NYSE) gap fill.

■ Learn what tools are used to identify and trade the gap fill, and learn how and when to execute the entry into the gap fill.

■ Gap Fills to Avoid

The first and most important fact about gap fills is that there are days that have a much lower probability for filling the gap. All of the following scenarios have this lower probability.

Options Expiration Fridays

Options expiration has a characteristic called *options max pain.* On option expiration days, the underlying stock price often moves toward a point that brings maximum loss to option buyers. Because of this, the market has a tendency to gap up and gap down and run away from its gap fill.

Rollover Thursday and the Day After

The futures market has what is called *contract rollover.* One futures contract ends and another begins each Thursday. For most futures markets, expiration day occurs on the third Friday of the month in the months of March, June, and September.

The First Trading Day of the New Quarter

The first trading day of a new quarter is historically a very strong bullish day. This strong up day is due to what some refer to as a *mutual fund Monday*. The beginning of a new quarter has a tendency to have a gap-up situation, and thus should be a day where the gap fill is avoided.

10-Point Gap-and-Go Levels

Opening 10 points above or below the previous day's close produces a professional gap-and-go situation. Many times a pro gap-up-and-go will gap up and rally the rest of the day. A 10-point gap-down-and-go is just the opposite. It will gap down and sell off the rest of the day. Recognizing these idiosyncrasies in the market will keep you from fighting gap fills that have a very low expectancy for filling their gap on the same day.

No-Trade Zones

No-trade zones are times in the markets that are consistently dangerous. Entering during these times has a low likelihood of successful trade. One of these no-trade zones is between 9:30 and 10 A.M. Eastern Time. It is also known as the first hour of the day. During this time, overnight price action has a tendency to whip stock traders around. In the process, traders are forced to close positions at the market, causing stop runs and shakeouts. Our opportunity to enter into the gap fill exists between 8 A.M. and 9:30 A.M. ET. This 90-minute window provides plenty of time to enter in the direction of the gap fill. After 9:30 A.M., the only thing a gap fill trade should do is take profit or manage an existing trade.

■ Gap Fill Percentages

Figure 12.1 shows a gap fill percentage for each day of the week for the past three years. You will notice that the gap fill has an average 70 percent gap fill on any given day. This is the number that traditional gap fill traders use as their win percentage. What about the other 30 percent of the time? That is where the 10 point gap-and-go comes in. As mentioned earlier, our gap fill rules let us trade the gap if it is less than 10 points away from where it would fill its gap. It stops us from trading gaps that don't have a statistical edge in filling the gap. The evidence for this rule is also in Figure 12.1. We will see

FIGURE 12.1 Gap Fill Statistics

A	B	C	D	E	F	G	H	I	J	K
2010	Monday	Tuesday	Wednesday	Thursday	Friday	TOTAL	Filled if Open < 10	Filled if Open > 10	Options Ex	1st Monthly Trading Day
Filled	33	34	34	34	37	172	161	11	7	4
Occurrences	47	52	52	51	50	252	207	45	12	12
Percent	70.2%	65.4%	65.4%	66.7%	74.0%	68.3%	77.8%	24.4%	58.3%	33.3%
2011	Monday	Tuesday	Wednesday	Thursday	Friday	TOTAL	Filled if Open < 10	Filled if Open > 10	Options Ex	1st Monthly Trading Day
Filled	23	34	33	34	31	155	136	19	7	6
Occurrences	46	52	52	51	51	252	180	72	12	12
Percent	50.0%	65.4%	63.5%	66.7%	60.8%	61.5%	75.6%	26.4%	58.3%	50.0%
2012	Monday	Tuesday	Wednesday	Thursday	Friday	TOTAL	Filled if Open < 10	Filled if Open > 10	Options Ex	1st Monthly Trading Day
Filled	32	36	40	38	30	176	173	3	7	6
Occurrences	47	50	51	51	52	251	217	34	12	12
Percent	68.1%	72.0%	78.4%	74.5%	57.7%	70.1%	79.7%	8.8%	58.3%	50.0%
2010–2012	Monday	Tuesday	Wednesday	Thursday	Friday	TOTAL	Filled if Open < 10	Filled if Open > 10	Options Ex	1st Monthly Trading Day
Filled	88	104	107	106	98	503	470	33	21	16
Occurrences	140	154	155	153	153	755	604	151	36	36
Percent	62.9%	67.5%	69.0%	69.3%	64.1%	66.6%	773.8%	21.9%	58.3%	44.4%

that for the past 3 years, if a gap is less than 10 points away from its gap fill, it has between a 77 percent and 79 percent chance of filling the gap.

Keeping records gives us a statistical edge and confidence to stick to our trading rules. Further evidence can be seen in Figure 12.1 for the professional gap-and-go rules. In the past three years, if price opened more than 10 points away from its gap fill, it had between an 8.8 percent and 26.4 percent chance of filling its gap. This gives traders confidence on a professional gap-and-go day to let the market go and not fight the gap fill. This little adjustment in trading rules changes the consistency of the gap fill considerably. It is also a detail that traditional gap fill traders often overlook.

Tools for the Gap Fill

To make it easier to trade the gap fill, there are a number of tools at our disposal. Many times, these tools are in the form of studies. In Figure 12.2, a study shows the 4 P.M. close of the previous day (the gap fill level). The

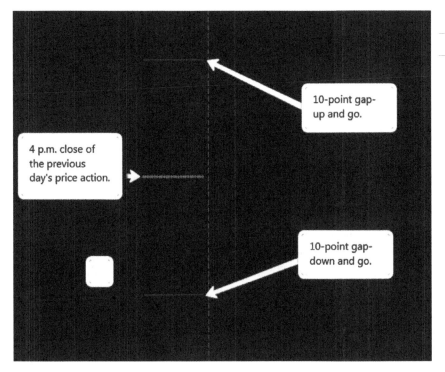

FIGURE 12.2 Pro Gap-and-Go Levels
Source: thinkorswim®.

same study shows the 10-point gap-and-go level above and below the gap fill. These levels can also be manually drawn in by first knowing the 4 P.M. close of the previous day's price action. Finding the 10-point gap-up and gap-down levels is just a matter of arithmetic.

The Traditional Trader's Way

Gap fill trading has evolved over the years. The futures pits in New York and Chicago started a self-fulfilling prophecy that we know today as the gap fill. The traditional way many traders learned to trade the gap in our electronic markets was much like the futures pit. The strategy was to enter at the opening bell using a market order. Many techniques advise to not use a stop, and to either exit at the gap fill as a profit target or close the trade at the end of the day. We know from gap fill percentage research that this type of strategy is incredibly dangerous. The days that the gaps don't fill end up being huge professional gap ups or gap downs. This technique emulated the pit, as traders used no stops and exited at the close if the gap did not fill. The theory behind such strategy was based on the statistics we covered above. They didn't have all the information to keep them from trading dangerous gap fills. Modern electronic trading has given our markets many more technical entries into these same gap fills. They allow us to use much tighter stops, which give the trader better risk-reward ratio.

The Conservative Way

The conservative way to enter into the gap fill is to use what we know about how measured moves (MMs) affect the market. Using the three entry strategies for retracements that we covered earlier, we have very specific and repeatable ways to enter in the direction of the gap fill. If we are *above* the gap fill and within the 10-point gap-up-and-go level, we look for resistance or a series of micros for an entry into the direction of the fill. If we are *below* the gap fill and within the 10-point gap-down-and-go level, we look for support or a series of micros for an entry into the direction of the fill. We use reduced-risk trades and stay in the trade until the gap is filled or a stop is hit.

■ The Gap Fill Workflow and Filter

Following is a mental checklist that a trader can use each morning to identify whether they have an opportunity to trade a gap fill.

If the answer is yes, move on to the next question. If the answer is no, do not trade the gap.

- Is it a day other than options ex, futures rollover, or the first trading day of a new month or quarter?

- Check the time. Are we within the 8 to 9:30 A.M. ET safe time to trade?

- Is the market inside the 10-point gap fill level?

- Has the market traded a large support or resistance level that could provide a change in trend or a micro next MM toward the gap fill?

If you answered yes to all of these questions, then you have a potential gap fill. You now have an opportunity to enter into a gap fill trade.

■ Entries

What can cause a reversal into a gap fill? Most gap fill entries originate from one of the following three levels:

1. *A 50 percent retracement.* Price action overnight will many times find its way to a 50 percent retracement. In Figure 12.3, price traded off of a 50 percent MM and formed a resistance level. This resistance level was used as an entry into the red gap fill line.
2. *A daily pivot.* Price action will also use the daily pivot for the next day as a support or resistance level that will lead into a gap fill.
3. *The 10-point gap-and-go.* The 10-point gap-and-go level has been well established as a resistance level. This trait allows traders to use it as an entry into the gap fill. There are countless days that the high or low of overnight price will be the 10-point mark.

Which Entry?

How do we enter into a position in the direction of the gap fill? We use the three entry strategies for retracements to enter into the gap fill. They rank in importance and priority:

1. The first test of resistance.
2. The second test methodology.
3. The series of micros after the trend break.

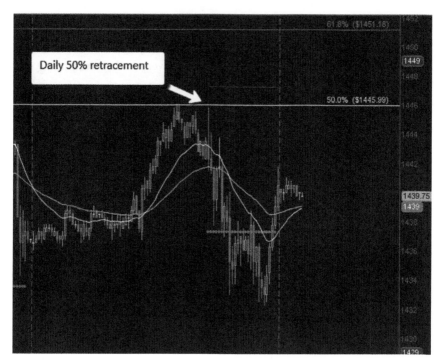

FIGURE 12.3 Reversal Point for a Gap Fill
Source: thinkorswim®.

The most common entry into the gap fill is the second test. Premarket price action is very technical and efficient. The majority of entries that present themselves are a retest of a support or resistance level that has already traded. Entering into the gap fill can be as simple as trading it with the second test strategy. We are always looking to trade in the direction of the gap fill level.

■ When Gaps Don't Fill

As with any trading strategy, the goal is to be prepared for any possible scenario. Being prepared gives us the advantage to know what to do and not be like a deer in headlights. One scenario is a more rare form of the gap fill. This scenario does not play by our 10-point gap-and-go rules. In this scenario, the market opens within the 10-point gap-and-go level. It will also give a nice clean uneventful premarket entry into the gap fill. The difference is that before the gap and profit targets are hit, a chain reaction of stops get hit and take out the gap fill trader's entry. This can happen during

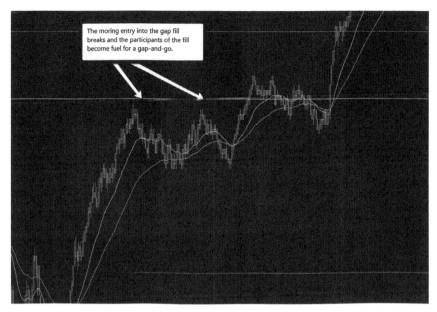

The moring entry into the gap fill breaks and the participants of the fill become fuel for a gap-and-go.

FIGURE 12.4 Broken Gap Fill Entry

Source: thinkorswim®.

the no-trade zone between 9:30 and 10 A.M. ET. Although it is rare, it can produce some of the biggest and most profitable gap fills that exist in the market. The most important thing to know is whether the market opened within or outside of its 10-point gap-and-go level. If it was within, it will fill its gap later on in the day.

In Figure 12.4, we see a morning entry into the gap fill that has broken. The participants of the entry into the gap fill become fuel for the breakout. Since the morning open price is within the 10-point gap-and-go, the gap has the potential of filling later on in the day.

■ What to Do?

Since this breakout is not a professional gap-and-go, we trade the series of MMs until the trend fails. A break in trend produces the first buy/sell signal back in the direction of the gap fill. A break in trend can be produced by one of two events:

1. A new high/low tick of the day can produce a reversal.
2. The pierce of a 61.8 percent level of the series of MMs.

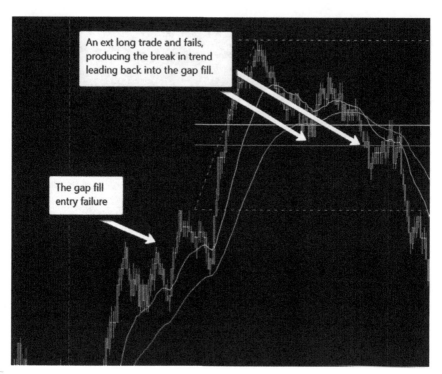

An ext long trade and fails, producing the break in trend leading back into the gap fill.

The gap fill entry failure

FIGURE 12.5 Gap Fill Entry Signal
Source: thinkorswim®.

Figure 12.5 shows the series of MMs later on that same day. The extension long trades and fails, producing a break in trend. This break in trend gives a trader his first sell signal back into the direction of the gap fill.

After the break of the extension long in Figure 12.5, the first sell signal is drawn as an MM short. In Figure 12.6 we see the new MM short giving the trader and entry back in the direction of the gap fill. Because this market opened within the 10-point gap-and-go level, it ended up filling its gap the same day. If the market had opened outside of the 10-point gap-and-go level, we would have expected the market to rally into the close as a professional gap-and-go day.

■ Why Is This Important to Your Trading?

By knowing and understanding the idiosyncrasies of the gap fill, traders have another consistent trade setup to count on for income. One thing to remember is that if you don't get an entry into the gap fill, there will always be

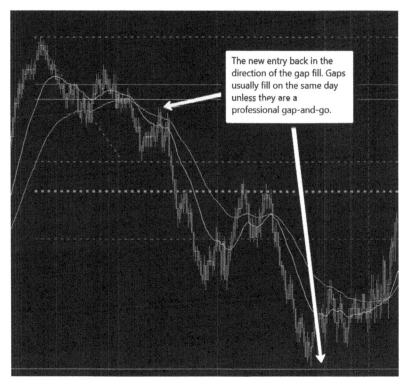

The new entry back in the direction of the gap fill. Gaps usually fill on the same day unless they are a professional gap-and-go.

FIGURE 12.6   Entry into the Gap Fill
Source: thinkorswim®.

another gap fill tomorrow. The gap fill is the most participated in of events in the ES futures markets. It has been a reliable trade for years, and will continue to be for years to come.

For more information, watch the video titled "Profiting from Gap Fills," available at http://eminiaddict.com/?p=5933.

CHAPTER 13

How to Manage Positions and Take Profits

Taking profit and managing a position are the two most important skills to be learned as a trader. There are a million ways to get into a trade. A systematic strategy for taking profit is in many ways much more important than an entry strategy. Sometimes the range in the market is very large. This large range means that the targets for normal measured moves (MMs) will be extremely large. The range is so large that it requires a trader to hold a position overnight. Newer traders who can't afford the overnight margin want to take smaller trades during the day. They also might not want to expose themselves to overnight volatility while they are asleep. The benefit of taking smaller profit targets inside of a larger MM is that a trader can be flat and have no risk at the end of the day. There are four ways to take profits inside of series of MMs.

■ The Rule for Measured Moves

There is a very simple rule for trading MMs. Each and every MM has its own unique entry and target: *take profit on the time frame you entered the trade on.*

All traders fall victim to fear and greed. Our systematic entry strategies help us keep fear in check. Taking profit at each MM's own unique target helps keep a trader from being a victim of greed. As you have witnessed, the –23 percent profit target is the exact reversal point at which a market turns. There are four ways to take profits inside a series of measured moves.

1. The distance formula
2. Trailing the series
3. After the confirmation of trend
4. The –23 percent profit target

■ The Distance Formula

The distance formula is for the short-term income–type trades. The distance formula is a small scalp-type trade and is the fastest way to take profit. The distance to its profit target is determined by the distance between the 50 and the 38.2 percent lines. The size of the trade depends on the size of the MM. The larger the MM, the larger the target will be. The distance formula can also be used as a first target on a trade in a series of MMs. You will find this strategy useful during the doldrums or slow times in the market.

In Figure 13.1, an MM short is trading. The entry is the 50 percent, but instead of using the –23 percent target, we used the 38.2 percent as the profit target. In the example, the distance between the 50 percent and the 38.2 percent line is 20 pips of profit.

You can also see that it trades that distance three times from its 50 percent line. During slow times in the market, levels like this will touch multiple times. It gives the trade the opportunity to profit on the same trade multiple times. Traditionally, the distance formula is best used on Friday afternoons and Monday mornings. The daily doldrums between 11:30 A.M. and 1:30 P.M. Eastern Time are also good times to use this strategy. The downside of the distance formula strategy is that unless you are trading multiple contracts, the move to the full –23 percent profit target is missed. The solution to this downside is discussed in Figure 13.2.

Figure 13.2 is another example of the distance formula. This time the distance formula is used to calculate the first target of a scaled out trade. In the example, the distance is 12 pips to the first target. This is similar to the standard scaling-out technique in that after the first target is hit, the stop is moved. The first target gives the trader extra room to stay in the trade without getting shaken out in a retest of entry. The best times to use this

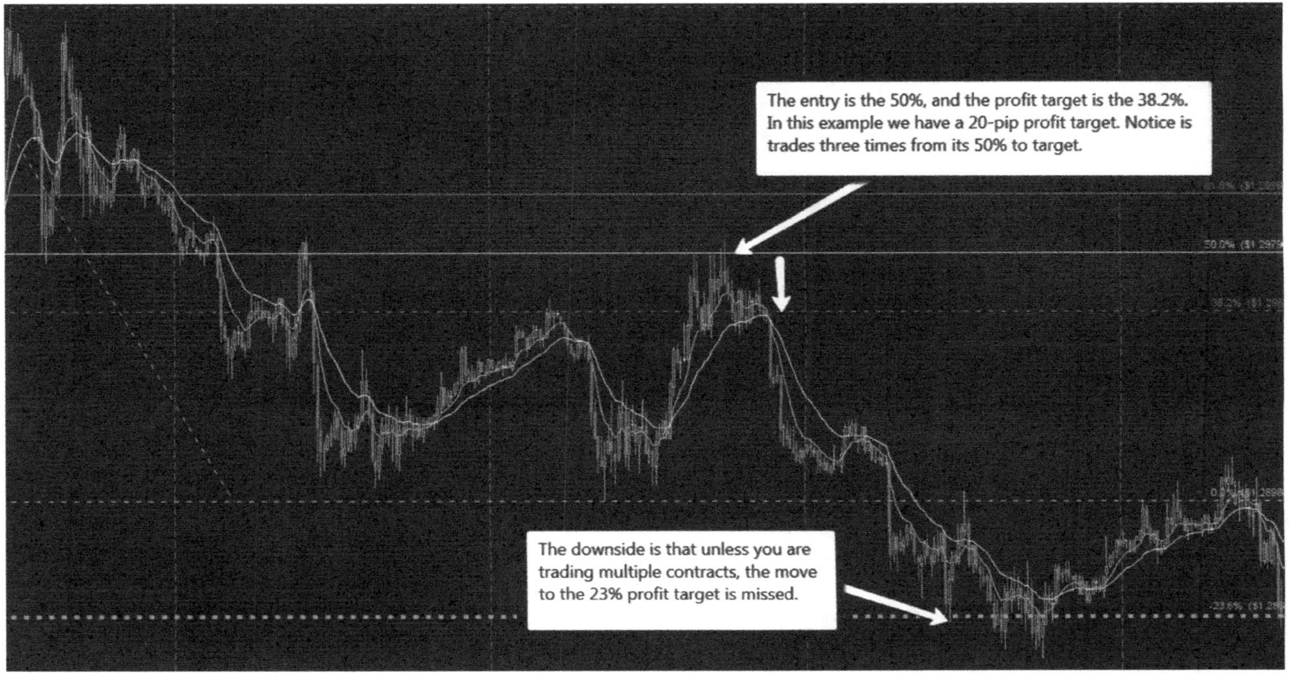

The entry is the 50%, and the profit target is the 38.2%. In this example we have a 20-pip profit target. Notice is trades three times from its 50% to target.

The downside is that unless you are trading multiple contracts, the move to the 23% profit target is missed.

FIGURE 13.1 Calculating the Distance Formula

Source: thinkorswim®.

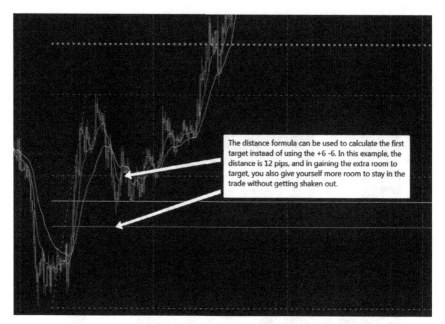

The distance formula can be used to calculate the first target instead of using the +6 -6. In this example, the distance is 12 pips, and in gaining the extra room to target, you also give yourself more room to stay in the trade without getting shaken out.

FIGURE 13.2 Finding First Target with Distance Formula
Source: thinkorswim®.

strategy are in extremely volatile markets. Volatile markets have very wide ranges and have the potential of stopping a trader out at the original entry. The benefit of a first target that is based on the distance formula is that the target is based on the range of the market. Larger setups give us larger first targets. Smaller setups give us smaller first targets. First targets based on the distance formula take the range and volatility of the day into account.

For more information, watch the video titled "The Distance Formula," available at http://eminiaddict.com/?p=5352.

■ Trailing a Series of Measured Moves

The series will help you stay in the trend. Trailing 61.8 percent levels is a way of maximizing profits. It allows a trader to stay in the larger trend to an MM's −23 percent target.

The rules for trailing a series include:

■ The trader trails the series of MMs until the 61.8 percent level fails. By trailing the series of MMs we maximize our entry and the risk-reward ratio of the trade.

- The trader must respect the normal progression of MMs. The progression of MMs trends in traditional MMs first. Traditional MMs can continue until the trend breaks the 61.8 percent level or until it blows past the trade's profit targets. After a trade has moved past its profit targets it starts to trade extensions. The 61.8 percent levels of the MM extensions must now be trailed. The progression is from traditional MMs to extension MMs, and if the extensions fail, the trend fails.

- If the series fails a 61.8 percent level, profit must be taken.

Figure 13.3 shows an example of a progression of MMs. An MM short has a target that is 300 pips away from its target. The entry to the MM short has moved away from its entry. We have the opportunity to trail the traditional MM's 61.8 percent level to maximize the trend. The trade continues its trend and moves past its profit target. The trend now starts a new

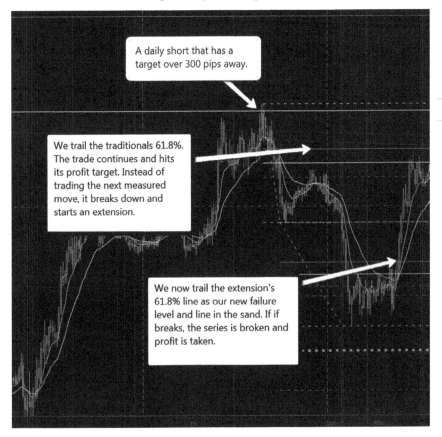

FIGURE 13.3 A Broken Series of Measured Moves
Source: thinkorswim®.

MM extension. We now trail the 61.8 percent level of the MM extension to maximize the trend. If it breaks the 61.8 percent level of the extensions, the trend will end and profit must be taken. Figure 13.3 shows that the MM extension has broken the series and profit has been taken.

■ After the Confirmation of Trend

The confirmation of trend will allow you to take small bites of bigger MMs. It is a technique for taking partial profit and confirming at larger trend.

In Figure 13.4, the arrows point to a MM's 50 percent retracement and its −23 percent profit target. In between the entry and the profit target are opportunities to take partial profit. A trader can also use this technique to add to an existing trade or even enter into a new position. An opposing MM is a trade setup that trades against or in opposition to the major trend.

In Figure 13.4 price breaks an opposing MM. This break of the opposing MM is a profit-taking opportunity. As soon as this opposing MM has broken, two things happen:

1. The main trend confirms its profit target.
2. A next MM is given as an entry opportunity.

Figure 13.5 is the progression of the next MM after the trend break. This next MM can be a brand new position, or an addition to the position that is already active. This next MM can be held to the larger MM's target.

■ Using the −23 Percent Profit Target: Take Profit on the Time Frame You Entered the Trade

The −23 percent is for intraday swing trades. We use a −23 percent target when a setup is too big to be hit by the end of the day. We can use the −23 percent target when intraday profits are more important than a swing trade or a long-term position. Each MM has its own unique target. If a trader is ever in doubt about taking profit or leaving a trade on, always take profit. There will always be another retracement or entry into the trend. There is a saying among traders: *There is no such thing as a missed trend.* There will always be another opportunity to enter. Taking profit and being flat the market gives the trader the opportunity to look for the next MM.

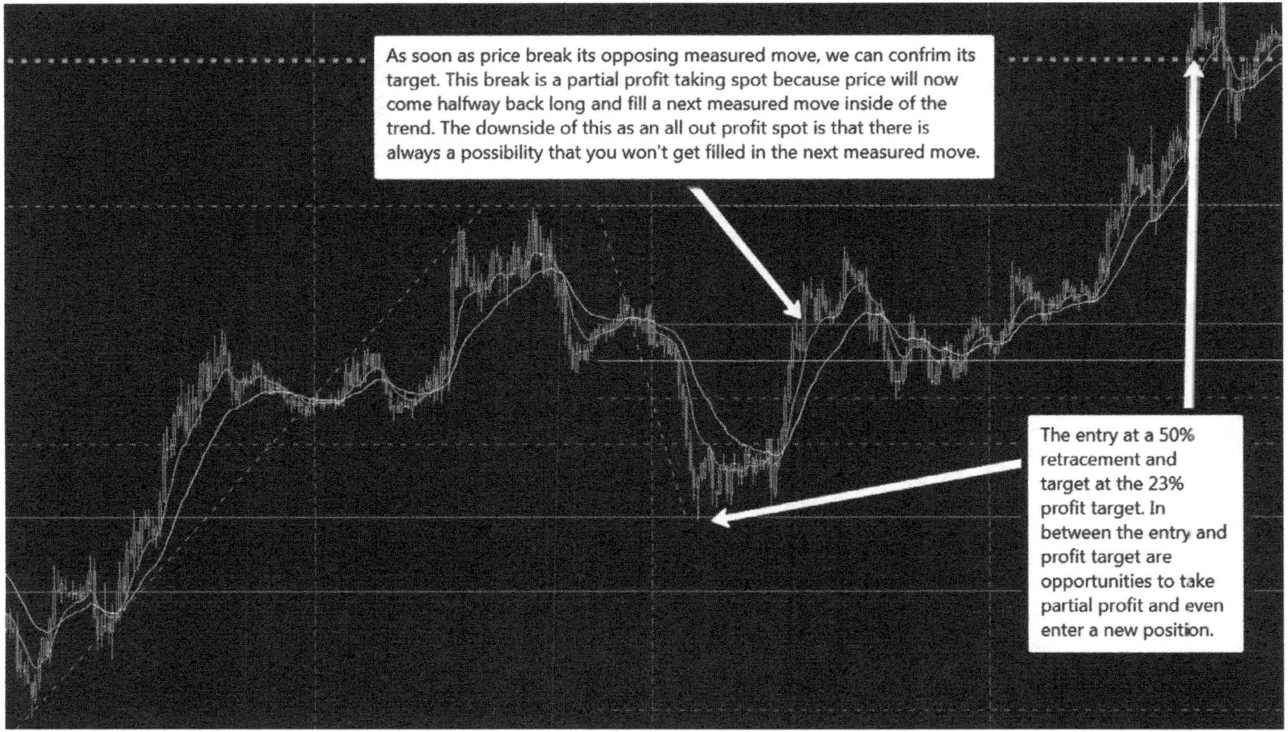

As soon as price break its opposing measured move, we can confirm its target. This break is a partial profit taking spot because price will now come halfway back long and fill a next measured move inside of the trend. The downside of this as an all out profit spot is that there is always a possibility that you won't get filled in the next measured move.

The entry at a 50% retracement and target at the 23% profit target. In between the entry and profit target are opportunities to take partial profit and even enter a new position.

FIGURE 13.4 Opposing Measured Move
Source: thinkorswim®.

HOW TO MANAGE POSITIONS AND TAKE PROFITS

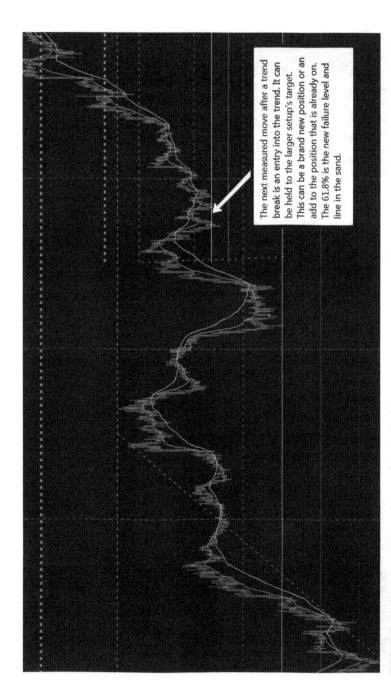

The next measured move after a trend break is an entry into the trend. It can be held to the larger setup's target. This can be a brand new position or an add to the position that is already on. The 61.8% is the new failure level and line in the sand.

FIGURE 13.5 Next Measured Move after Trend Break

Source: thinkorswim®.

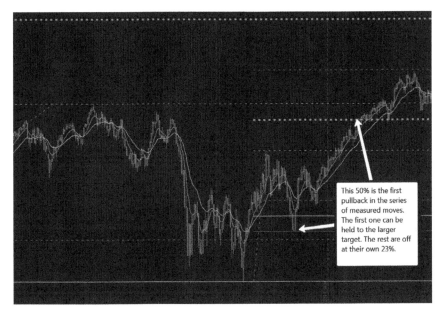

FIGURE 13.6 First Measured Move after a Trend Break

Source: thinkorswim®.

Figure 13.6 is an example of a 50 percent MM that is trading in a series. The first pullback has an opportunity of trading to a much larger target. A trader can decide to take profit on the time frame he or she entered the trade. These are the moments that we as traders have to deal with fear and greed. Taking profit on the time frame you entered the trade kills the greed. A trader takes profit at a profit target, and moves on to other trade setups.

▪ Why Is This Important to Your Trading?

Having strategies to enter the market in a systematic way is one of the very first steps in becoming a rule-based trader. Having systematic strategies to exit the market with profit is just as important. Sometimes a series of MMs might not complete during the day before the close of the market. Strategies allow us to maximize our profit and stay in a trend until it breaks. Staying in a trend as it continues in a series of MMs allows us to maximize our profit. It also helps us maximize our risk-reward ratios.

Here are some things to remember about each of the profit-taking strategies.

- The distance formula is for the short-term income–type trades. Use the distance formula in slow choppy markets. Friday afternoons and Monday mornings are notorious for their slow, choppy sessions.

- The series will help you stay in the trend. Trail a series of measured moves when the market is trending. Tuesday through Thursday, markets are usually in trends.

- The confirmation of trend will allow you to take small bites of big setups. Extended ranges and large setups require smaller bites or profit targets. Use opposing MMs that fail to confirm trends, and take partial profit in trades.

- The traditional –23 percent is for intraday swing trades. Each and every MM has its own unique target. No trader has ever gone broke taking profit.

Many traditional traders consider taking profits an art form. In the modern age of algorithms and technical markets, profit taking can become completely mechanical.

For more information, watch the video titled "How to Manage Positions and Take Profits," available at http://eminiaddict.com/?p=6007.

CHAPTER 14

Risk Management (Advanced Trade Management)

Money management is where traders make their biggest mistakes when beginning their trading careers. Not using stops on every trade, risking large amounts, and overtrading are some of the biggest mistakes newer traders make. We're going to address these issues and share trading rules to conquer those mistakes.

■ Bob the Trader

Let's use a story about a hypothetical trader named Bob. Bob just started trading and recently found some new indicators that are extremely accurate at picking turning points in the market. Bob knows that he should use stops on all of his trades. The problem Bob is having is that when he uses stops, he seems to get shaken out of all his trades. It feels like he's always getting stopped out even though he is correct about the direction of the market. Bob decides that he's going to start making trades but not use his stops.

Bob is also struggling with how much he should risk on each and every trade. He knows he should limit his risk to a fixed percentage of his account value. At the risk percentage that he is supposed to use, he feels that his account is growing very slowly. Bob seems to find excitement in the markets only when he is overleveraging himself. Instead of approaching markets in a systematic away, he begins a dangerous spiral into gambling. His need for excitement outweighs common sense and rational thought.

Bob also finds himself moving from one instrument to another. He knows he should stick to just a couple of instruments and learn them extremely well, but Bob feels that the instruments that are extremely reliable and consistent don't move enough for him. He searches hundreds of stocks every single night looking for opportunities. Bob has also found that he likes to trade stocks that have news announcements because they move farther and faster.

One of the worst things that could ever happen to a trader happens to Bob. It works—at first.

Bob's rule-breaking, overleveraging, overtrading strategies reward him. Being rewarded for this extremely risky behavior is one of the worst things that can happen to a trader. All of this bad behavior is now reinforced. Using stops is now associated with pain, and not using stops is associated with profit and pleasure. Trading instruments that move consistently but slowly is boring to Bob. Trading instruments during news events that are extremely volatile is associated with excitement and pleasure. Bob also associates risking large amounts of his account with quicker rewards and pleasure. Bob continues to risk larger and larger portions of his account. These types of early mistakes can be a death sentence to a beginning trader. To put it in the simplest terms possible, imagine giving your dog a treat every time it pooped or peed on your family room carpet. The dog is going to continue to do what he is rewarded for. Bob will also continue to make the same mistakes that he was initially rewarded for. It will not matter how much pain is associated with his behavior in the future because some of his first experiences were extremely powerful and pleasurable events. It is only a matter of time before all of these extremely risky behaviors catch up with Bob. It only takes one bad trade to end his trading career forever.

One weekday morning Bob wakes up to find one of his favorite instruments in a steep decline. While listening to CNN, he hears bad news about this particular company. He decides to sell at the market and not wait for a retracement to enter into a position. Later that day he is well into profits and decides to hold his trade overnight. As usual, Bob does not use stops, is overleveraged, and has been rewarded for his bad behavior in the past. To his amazement, the next morning this company's earnings announcement comes back positive. This was exactly the opposite of what all the news announcements said was going to happen. Bob is at a significant loss and is extremely distraught about his "bad luck." Instead of closing his position, he decides that he will average into it. If yesterday was a great time to sell it, today at higher prices is an even better time to get into and add to a position. He continues to add to the position moving against him in increasingly larger and more damaging amounts. When Bob has finally had enough, he closes his position at a significant loss, determined to make his losses back.

Bob is now on a rampage. Instead of risking smaller amounts as his account would dictate, he is risking larger and larger amounts so a big payoff can help him break even. Bob finally decides that he isn't cut out for trading and closes his account.

Bob's is an incredibly painful story, and it should paint a picture of what not to do. There are a couple of things that every new trader should realize before starting:

- Trading is a job. Treat is like a job and not like a game.

- Trading can be extremely boring if your position is sized correctly.

- Trading is not gambling. Go to Vegas if you want to gamble. (Most traders, if given the opportunity, do not like to gamble—especially when they know the risk versus reward.)

■ Curtis the Contractor

Certain types of individuals can make the transition into becoming a trader much easier. These types of individuals have had to deal with risk and reward in the real world. These individuals might include anyone that has owned a business or been self-employed. These individuals might have had to pay for advertisements to gain customers. Or, for example, if one were a contractor, he would have to consider transportation and building materials as costs of a potential job. Someone that has been a W2 employee his entire life must be able to adopt this sense of risk versus reward.

Let's look at an example of risk versus reward in the real world. Curtis is a contractor who has just won bids for two different jobs that are on opposite sides of town. Job A is farther away than Job B. Curtis has calculated his transportation costs and cannot account for rising gas prices over the time that this job will take to be completed. Both jobs have about the same profit, but Job A will take more from his bottom line, and in turn is less desirable. Curtis also has to pay his workers for the time they spend on the road driving to a job that is farther away from his company's headquarters. Job B is a couple of miles away. He can keep track of his workers more efficiently when they're closer to the office. Transportation costs will be much lower on Job B. Curtis chooses Job B.

Business owners and self-employed individuals have an automatic risk-reward ratio analysis built into them. This is an incredibly important trait that new traders will have to train themselves to do quickly and efficiently. The saying *it takes money to make money* applies here.

■ Risk per Trade

Risk per trade is calculated based on the percentage of trading account size. A good starting point for risk percentage is 1 percent risk per trade. This is low enough to allow you to still make mistakes, and large enough to profit when a trade works in your favor. The reason that we use a fixed amount is so that our results are consistent. Different types of individuals will have different feelings on what is too much or too little risk. An individual who was born with a silver spoon in his or her mouth might not think that 1 percent is risk enough to make it worth his or her time. Someone who was raised in a less fortunate household and understands the value of the dollar might have trouble risking the full 1 percent. It all depends on the account size. If you start with a small account, you risk a small amount. If you start with a large account, you still risk 1 percent and are correctly position sized. Risk per trade is the single most important ingredient to having a long and lasting trading career.

■ How Many Futures Contracts Should I Trade?

Knowing your risk per trade percentage is yet only part of the equation. To be correctly sized for a trade, a trader also needs to know what size stop-loss to use. He or she also needs to know what the instrument is worth per pip or per tick. Figure 14.1 is an example of a position-sizing calculator for the

Variables		
Account size	$40,000.00	
% of Portfolio at risk	1%	6.00 Contracts
Stop loss in pips	12	
$ value per pip	$5.00	

FIGURE 14.1 YM Position-Sizing Calculator

Variables

Account size	$40,000.00	
% of Portfolio at risk	1%	5.00 Contracts
Stop loss in pips	6	
$ value per pip	$12.50	

FIGURE 14.2 ES Position-Sizing Calculator

E-mini Dow futures contract (YM). A $40,000 account, risking 1 percent per trade, with a 12-tick stop-loss, at a value of $5 per tick, can buy or sell six futures contracts.

Figure 14.2 is an example of a position-sizing calculator for the E-mini S&P futures contract (ES). The same $40,000 account, risking 1 percent per trade, with a six-tick stop, at a value of $12.50 per tick, can buy or sell five futures contracts.

Figure 14.3 is an example of a position-sizing calculator for the E-micro Forex futures contract (M6E).

The account balance is much smaller, with a total of $3000. At 1 percent risk, with 12 pip stops and a value of $1.25 per pip, a trader can trade two contracts. This means even very small accounts have the ability to trade multiple contracts.

■ Stop Placement

Most traders start out trading stocks. What most part traders don't realize is that stocks are a place to park money. Stocks are not the best place to trade. The most efficient places to trade are futures contracts. Futures contracts allow for trading platforms with "advanced trade management." This is the ability to take profit at predetermined levels automatically without a trader's input. They are predefined and executed automatically. These

Variables

Account size	$3,000.00	
% of Portfolio at risk	1%	2.00 Contracts
Stop loss in pips	12	
$ value per pip	$1.25	

FIGURE 14.3 M6E Position-Sizing Calculator

"advanced trade management" features allow us to create profiles that we classify into two different groups. These two different groups are called the reduced-risk trade and free trade.

Trading stocks can be much more stressful than trading futures. Most stocks require larger stops due to their inefficiency and lack of participation. Because of these wider stops, stock traders are often forced to sit in trades for extended periods of time. The lack of movement keeps the trade at or around a trader's original entries. It can last for days, or however long it takes for the stock to move away from your entry. One characteristic of stocks versus futures is that stocks seem to chop around their entries. Futures quickly move away from their entries from support or resistance levels with high levels of participation.

■ The Free Trade

The free trade works by trading instruments in multiples of two contracts. We use the even number so we can scale out of half of the trade. We start with a −12-pip stop and a +6-pip first target. As soon as the +6-pip first target is hit, the advanced trade management system moves our −12-pip stop to −6. Now you have a free trade. The worst-case scenario from this point forward is that you get stopped out at breakeven. Your only cost associated with this trade is any slippage and commissions.

■ The Reduced-Risk Trade

The reduced-risk (RR) trade works by trading instruments in multiples of two contracts. We again use the even number so we can scale out of half of the trade. We start with a −6-tick stop and a +2-tick first target. As soon as the +2-tick first target is hit, the advanced trade management system moves our −6-tick stop to −4. Now you have an RR trade. The worst-case scenario from this point forward is that you get stopped out with a −2-tick loss plus any slippage and commission.

■ Why Scale Out?

Scaling out of positions isn't right for everyone. What it allows a trader to do is quickly find out if a trade is going to work or not. It limits the amount of time and anxiety in the first moments of a trade. A stock trade might take days to move away from an entry. The free-trade methodology takes seconds to get its first target. After the first target is hit, it becomes a free trade. The anxiety is now gone, and the trader can wait either for the profit target to be hit or to be stopped out at breakeven on the trade. A trader has lost nothing and now can look for another entry.

Pick an Instrument and Focus on It

Newer traders have a tendency to want to look at hundreds of stocks. The rationale behind this comes from the need to want to find the perfect setup. Trading firms like Goldman Sachs, Morgan Stanley, and UBS have experts for each specific instrument. As a trader, your goal should be to become an expert at the trading instrument you choose to trade.

Trading the News Is Gambling

The goal of the trader should not be to trade the news but to avoid its volatility. News announcements that affect the market are scheduled every single day. Your job the night before is to know when and what those news announcements are. Traders are not necessarily concerned about what the news is or whether it is good or bad. Experienced traders care only when the news events occur so they can avoid them. It is not the news that is important; it is the reaction to the news.

Why Is This Important to Your Trading?

Understanding the principles in this chapter will help you avoid the single most common mistake new traders make. In the futures market it is said that over 90 percent of traders fail. If that number is true you could guess that of that 90 percent of them were overleveraged. Being overleveraged is the single biggest reason traders fail to succeed. In the modern age of trading there is no reason to be overleveraged. There are now futures contracts available that trade for as little as $1.25 per pip. Before the smaller contracts existed, a new trader was forced to be overleveraged with a smaller account. Most new traders start with smaller accounts. It might be all the trader can afford, or perhaps he is just dipping his toe in the water to see what the futures market is like. The ability to trade with smaller accounts makes entry to futures trading more accessible to beginner traders.

You might hear a new trader say that it seems like a waste of time when they are correctly position-sized. Ironically, the feeling of boredom and the lack of excitement is when you know you are correctly position-sized. This is the moment a trader realizes that trading is a job. Trading, just like any other job, can be mindlessly boring. The trading career is a marathon, not a sprint. A trader's best allies are discipline and patience. Just like muscles, as discipline and patience are exercised and cultivated over time, they grow stronger. Set yourself up for success correctly from the beginning and be part of the 10 percent that succeed. Never break your risk management rules.

CHAPTER 15

The Inner Trader

The Emotions of a Trader

Traders face a wide variety of emotions throughout the trading day. Emotions such as fear, greed, euphoria, and anxiety can make you a victim if you do not take control of them. A great trader should have a grasp of math and probabilities. The ability to calculate risk-reward ratios and quickly determine if the trade is worth taking is incredibly important.

■ Mentality

A common mistake that the new trader makes is approaching the market with the gambler's mentality. The correct way to approach trading is to think of oneself as a casino. The casino has hundreds of gamblers that walk into its doors, and it knows that the more hands of cards it deals, the larger its stake will be at the end of the night. A casino has a statistical advantage over the gamblers. A trader with an edge, sound money management practices, and specific trading rules also has that same statistical edge over the market. A great trader knows, just like the casinos, that if he follows his trading rules and applies his edge to the market, over time he will come out ahead profitable at the end of the day.

A trader also has to have heart. The trader not only has to know what trade setups to trade, but also has to have the ability and confidence to take the setups. Some traders know what to do, but they do not have the confidence to take the setups that they know are important to be profitable at the end of the day. There are a couple of reasons why these traders might not have the confidence to take the trades they know they should. Traders might feel that the trade that is setting up is too scary. The main cause of this fear is that they risk too much per trade. Most traders are too terrified about losing and whether the setup will work out or not. Traders should not focus so much on whether a trade setup works or not. Newer traders are so worried about losing that they are unable to trade the setups that are profitable to their bottom line. Great traders have confidence that mathematically they might lose on a trade setup here and there, but that their edge executed over time is profitable. Traders should focus on their statistical advantage and know that making the right decision over the long run will work out to their benefit. It is not the instant gratification of winning that is important. It is about making the right decisions over time that allows you to be profitable at the end. Great traders also need to be very proficient at analyzing patterns, such as repeated successful times of the day to trade. Patterns of losses can also develop. Traders need to be able to identify those patterns, learn from them, and then profit from them.

■ Money Management

One of the most overlooked but important facets of a trader's plan are his money management behaviors. It is the downfall and the cause of most of the problems that a newer trader will face. Most traders come into the market undercapitalized and risking too much money per trade. This makes them worry whether each and every trade setup will work. Money management is the difference between being the casino and being the gambler. If a trader comes into the market undercapitalized and risking too much money per trade, he becomes the gambler. This undercapitalization causes the fear, anxiety, and inability to take the trade setups that will add to his bottom line. Most of these undercapitalized traders know what they should be doing but are afraid to do it. Correcting their money management practices allows a trader to take the setups that matter and not be so concerned about each and every individual trade setup's outcome.

Traders have to know when to use their capital and when to lower the risk when it is needed. There are some days of the week that require lower risk than others. There are events inside of our market that create extremely volatile price action. Newer traders look at these extremely volatile events as opportunities to trade and end up overleveraged and gambling their money. Experienced traders know to stay out of the market during these volatile and inconsistent times to preserve their capital. If experienced traders trade these events, they do so with reduced size and are extremely risk averse. The difference between these two traders is one has a gambler's mentality (i.e., the newer trader). The other has the casino's mentality (i.e., profiting over time with a statistical advantage). This is the difference between being reactive and proactive.

News events create reactive traders that are opening and closing positions based on emotion. The measured move (MM) is based on accumulation. Computer algorithms accumulate positions based on patterns in the market that give specific targets for trades. There is nothing wrong with being in a position before the news and profiting from an event. That is what the algorithms and experienced traders attempt to do. Newer traders have a tendency to not be in a position before the news and still want to trade the reaction. Some traders never realize the danger of these events. Traders can end up erasing all of their hard-earned gains for a day or week by trying to trade it.

■ Emotions

Traders cannot profit from every trade that they take. This requires traders to have strong control over their emotions. They must have the confidence and knowledge that the mathematics behind their trading strategy favors a positive outcome. Knowledge that every trade can't be a winner allows traders to have control over their emotions. Even after a bad trade, control allows the trader to move on and to continue to make good decisions going forward. Great traders know that making those good decisions over time will give them their statistical advantage. Successful traders know how to work with the skills that they have and to recognize the trades they should be taking. They also recognize dangerous times in the market and trades that they should avoid.

Combining these skills with smart money management and emotional control is the key. What most traders have the hardest time with is managing their emotions. As it turns out, emotions are extremely difficult to manage when money management skills are poor. Risking too much of your capital in any one trade will create emotions that lead to bad decisions.

Poor Money Management + High Levels of Emotion = Bad Decisions
Strong Money Management + Controlled Emotions = Good Decisions

Bad decisions turn into bad trades and good decisions end up being profitable trades. As a trader, if you ever feel that your emotions are high, the first step is to reduce your risk. Many traders may say that this is a waste of time. They feel that the excitement is gone, and they are bored, but that lower emotional state they are experiencing is where good decisions are made.

If you want excitement, go to Vegas and gamble. What's interesting about good traders is that if you put them in a situation where they have the opportunity to gamble, they will choose not to. Great traders know that the odds are stacked in the casino's favor. There is not a successful trader in the world that will knowingly throw away his money on odds that are not in his favor. Once a newer trader makes this mentality shift from a gambler to casino, he will never want to be the gambler again. Money management and emotional control go hand in hand. Being able to move on after a bad trade, both emotionally and financially, allows a trader to make good decisions moving forward. Being able to move on after a bad trade comes only from being positioned sized correctly.

■ How Long Does It Take for a New Trader to Trade Well?

Malcolm Gladwell's book *Outliers* (Little, Brown and Co., 2008) makes the case that 10,000 hours of practice at anything will make you an expert. The saying *practice makes perfect* should be changed to *perfect practice makes perfect*. Following trading rules consistently will produce consistent results. Following trading rules inconsistently will produce inconsistent results. Traders should be constantly focused on how to become better at behaving properly during times of uncertainty. A newer trader will be scared to take a trade setup, and an experienced trader will be afraid not to take that same trade setup.

I'm sure you've heard people complain about their bad luck. Their bad luck could be associated with finances, relationships, hobbies, or just life in general. A healthy trader's mentality forces him or her to acknowledge that there is no such thing as good or bad luck. What others mistake for luck is where preparation meets opportunity. The trader has to be prepared to see the opportunities that the market presents. The opportunities a prepared trader sees will be completely invisible to the unprepared. Once you recognize these patterns in the market, a whole new world of opportunity opens up.

It is also important to recognize the reality that no matter how good a trader is at recognizing opportunities and executing his or her plan, it will never be completely perfect. Because of the nature of trading, no trader will be unable to go without losing on some trades. It is the law of probabilities. Some trades will be winners; some trades will be losers. What safeguards do traders have to protect themselves? Statistical edge, sound money management practices, and a consistent profit-taking strategy will make the winners outpace the losers. Following trading rules and having strong control over one's emotions will help in times of uncertainty.

■ Attitude

Most new traders focus on all the bad things that can happen to them while they're trading. These traders imagine that there are malicious forces at work or individuals in the market that are out to get them. The simple fact is that our worst enemy is ourselves. Focusing on bad things that can happen during a trade gives us zero positive results. Having positive expectations for a trade will lead to positive results. Having a bad attitude or a negative expectation for a trade, whether it works or not, makes it impossible to learn from mistakes if they are made. If a trade meets your requirements and you follow your rules entering into that trade setup, there's no reason to be ashamed or upset if it doesn't work out. If a trade doesn't work out the way you thought it would, the most important thing to do is to analyze why it didn't work—be proactive for the next round. If it met all of your trading rules and it didn't work out in your favor, chalk it up to statistics and move on to the next opportunity. If you find that it didn't meet your criteria for the trade, learn from the mistake and do not make the same mistake twice. You can become a better trader from the information that you gained from the loss. Do not complain or worry about things that are outside of your control as a trader. You cannot control the market; you can control only how you react to what happens.

Are You Proactive or Reactive?

There are certain times in the market that a trader needs to be extremely careful or not trade at all. These times are news announcements, government rate decisions, and breaking news. A great trader always knows when these news announcements take place prior to the bell ringing for a new day. Knowing when the news announcements happen allows traders to be out of the market or managing a position they are already in. Where newer traders might see these as opportunities to trade, experienced traders know that these events create unreliable trade setups.

Unreliable trade setups represent a danger to one's account. Ninety percent of the time the market trades in reliable predictable and logical measured moves. The other 10 percent of the time price action is unreliable and the patterns in the market make no sense at all. This is caused by a proactive trade and a reactionary trade. Proactive trades are planned; reactive trades are created by emotions. Our job as traders is to trade the 90 percent of the time that the market trades in predictable and logical MMs. Trading with MMs allows us to plan our entries with specific profit targets well ahead of time. An MM can set up hours, days, or even weeks ahead of time. This information gives us an ability to understand the risk-reward ratio. Professional traders are proactive in their approach to trading.

Inexperienced traders are reactive in their approach to trading. Inexperienced traders will want to chase a trade that has already started. Professional traders will see it well ahead of time and be in the trade, moving toward its profit target. Adopting the professional trader's mindset is easy to do. All a trader has to do is to refuse to trade an unplanned MM. If a trade isn't planned, it isn't rated. There is a saying traders use: *If you see the move and you're not in it, the trade is over*. If you refuse to chase the market and trade only planned MMs, you are well under way to becoming a great trader. Chasing a trade that wasn't planned puts a trader in a reactive trade situation. Most new traders feel that they're constantly chasing the market. They know the market moves, but they do not understand why. When inexperienced traders chase the market, professionals that originated the MM are already taking profits. These chased trades are fuel for the next MM. This next MM is also initiated by those professional traders. The battle that is going on in the market is fought between the professional proactive traders and the inexperienced reactive traders. There is a very small group of professionals and a very large group of the inexperienced. This small group of professional traders trade with huge size and need the liquidity of the futures markets. The large group of inexperienced traders trade with smaller size but provide much of the fuel that drives the reactionary trades in the market. The few take advantage of the many. Once a trader has adopted trading rules and a consistent workflow, he can focus on trading well. If a trader is following his or her rules, they will be profitable.

■ Trading Well versus Trading for Profit and Emotional Capital

All traders are trading to make money. It is incredibly important as a trader to be focused on trading well versus trading to make profit. When a trader is focused on the dollar amount of the trade, his emotions can get the best of him. Monetary values mean different things to different people. To keep the amount of money being traded from becoming an emotional situation, some traders will actually go as far as to change their depth of market from dollars to ticks. Changing from dollars to ticks allows them to ignore that monetary value of the trade and focus on trading the MM from its entry to its profit target. When money is involved, traders get emotional.

Trading well means following a predefined list of trading rules *to a tee*. Experienced traders know that if a trade will be profitable in the end, a trader must trade every single MM that meets the criteria of a successful trade. Trading rules such as not trading the first half-hour of the market open keeps a trader from making reactionary trades. Emotional capital is the confidence a trader has in his system and rules. In many ways, emotional capital is much more important than the size of the trader's account. A trader gains emotional capital or confidence only by executing his plan successfully day in and day out. Even the very experienced trader's emotional capital can be fragile. If a trader makes a bad decision and the outcome is a loss, it can damage his emotional capital. When emotional capital is affected, it could keep that trader from executing his plan to the best of his ability. We need to keep a positive attitude and treat our emotional capital with as much care and attention as our monetary capital. Traders who have had a blow to their confidence might not take the next trade that their trading rules tell them is important to take.

One exercise a trader must repeat every single day after the close is to go back to the charts and review the opportunities the day presented. A trader who followed his trading rules to a tee would've had an amazing day. This gives the trader confidence to come into the next trading day executing his or her plan.

Confidence and positive expectations are a prerequisite to trading well and being profitable. Trading MMs requires specific entries with very specific profit targets. There is no room for hesitation when executing a trade setup. Negative expectations and bad attitudes will prevent a trader from executing his or her plan. Confidence, positive attitudes, and positive expectations give traders confidence to execute, which leads to profitable results. There is a quote by Admiral William Halsey that says: *Touch a thistle timidly, and it pricks you; grasp it boldly, and its spines crumble*. It is a great quote for life, but it also applies to trading. Trading the MM requires a lack of hesitation and an ability to commit. Do not wait timidly and end up chasing a trade with uncertainty. Make sure all the rules and conditions are met, and trade fully planned measured moves with confidence.

■ The Phases of Measured Moves

It is incredibly important to understand what happens inside of each and every MM. There are four phases that each MM goes through. These phases repeat until the cycle is broken. Once a cycle is broken, the four phases of MM's begin in the opposite direction.

The Four Phases of Measured Moves

1. The first phase is the entry into the trade at the 50 percent MM. The first phase has to stay within the 61.8 percent level in order to continue its cycle.
2. The second phase is the time in the trade between the entry and previous high or low of the MM.
3. The third phase is the time in the trade between the previous high or low and the profit target of the MM.
4. The fourth phase is the profit target of the entire MM. The fourth phase will stop at the MM's profit target and retrace into the next MM in the series.

The signal for the continuation of the series of MMs is the defense of the 61.8 percent line inside of the next MM in the series. The signal for a trend reversal is the break of the 61.8 percent line.

The four phases of MMs are illustrated in Figure 15.1. Phases of bullish MMs continue over and over as long as buyers are in control. Buyers remain in control by continuing to defend the 61.8 percent line in each subsequent bullish MM. When buyers are in control, the demand is greater than the supply. This greater demand results in a price that continues to rise. Prices will continue to rise as long as the 61.8 percent line continues to hold.

If the 61.8 percent line should ever fail, a new phase of bearish MMs begins. The new phase of bearish MMs will continue over and over as long as sellers remain in control. Sellers remain in control by continuing to defend the 61.8 percent line in each subsequent bearish MM. When sellers are in control supply is greater than demand. This greater supply results in a price that continues to decline. Prices will continue to decline as long as the 61.8 percent line continues to hold.

Figure 15.1 illustrates what happens when a 61.8 percent line fails. The moment that a phase 1 entry fails to trade to its target, and breaks the 61.8 percent line, the trend of the market goes from buyers to sellers. The long cycle ends and begins a short cycle that continues to repeat until the next 61.8 percent line failure.

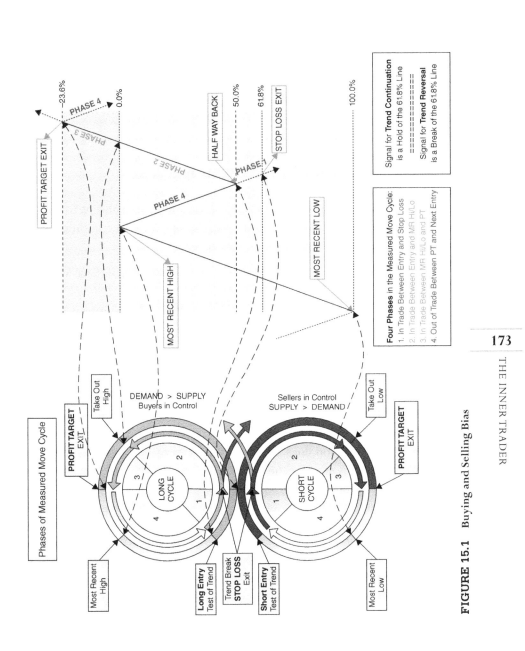

FIGURE 15.1 Buying and Selling Bias

THE INNER TRADER

■ The Series of Measured Moves

The progression of MMs continues in a systematic way in all highly liquid trading instruments. In these examples, we are talking about markets that are moving higher in bullish MMs. These patterns also exist in markets that are moving lower in bearish MMs. There is a mantra that makes this progression easy to remember: *The markets trade from traditionals, to extensions, to straight up*. Figure 15.2 is an example of how a series of MMs develops.

■ Basic Traditional Measured Moves

The progression of measured moves is the most important concept to remember. The series of MMs begins with a traditional MM. The traditional MM can continue until one of three things happen:

1. The traditional MM hits its target and retraces into the next traditional MM.
2. The traditional MM fails a 61.8 percent level.
3. The traditional MM breaks out of a profit target. Once a traditional MM breaks out of its target it becomes an extension.

Extension Measured Moves

The extension MM can continue until one of three things happen:

1. The extension MM hits its target and retraces in the next extension MMs. If the extension does not break out of its profit target the same most recent low is used for the next extension.
2. The extension MM fails a 61.8 percent level.
3. The extension MM breaks out of a profit target. Once an extension breaks out of its profit target it starts a new extension.

Extension Measured Moves

There is a general rule that helps to remember what to do with extension MMs. *The market must continue to go straight up in extensions, or not at all*. If extensions break, the trend breaks. Extension MMs can continue until one thing happens:

1. An expanded extension fails a 61.8 percent level.

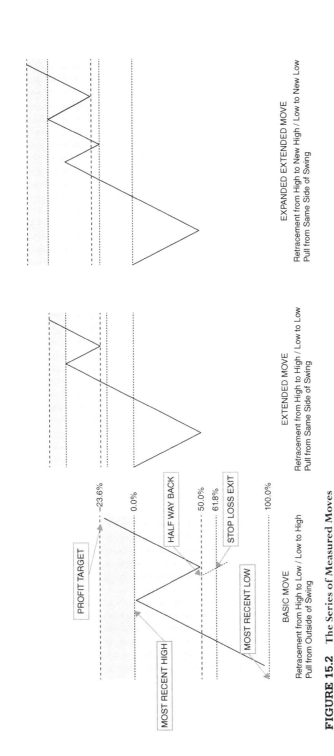

FIGURE 15.2 The Series of Measured Moves

BASIC MOVE
Retracement from High / Low to High
Pull from Outside of Swing

EXTENDED MOVE
Retracement from High to High / Low to Low
Pull from Same Side of Swing

EXPANDED EXTENDED MOVE
Retracement from High to New High / Low to New Low
Pull from Same Side of Swing

PROFIT TARGET

MOST RECENT HIGH

HALF WAY BACK

STOP LOSS EXIT

MOST RECENT LOW

-23.6%

0.0%

50.0%

61.8%

100.0%

FIGURE 15.3 The Measured Move Flow Chart

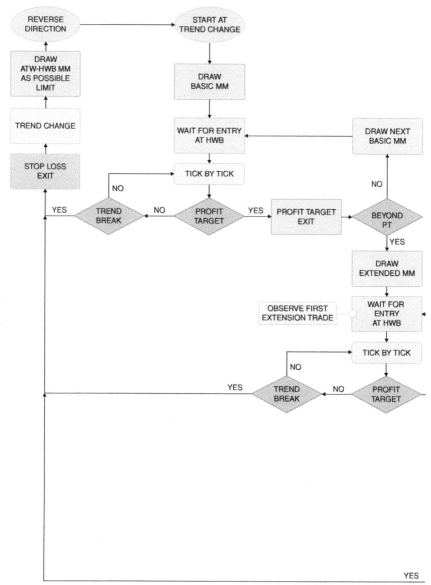

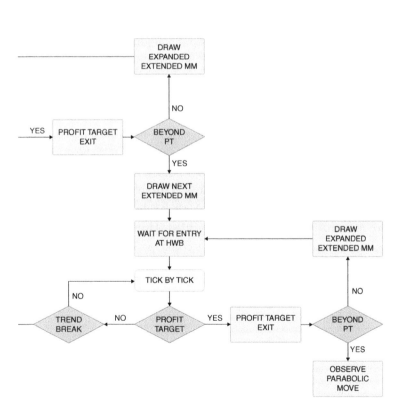

■ The Progression of Measured Moves

In Figure 15.3, the measured move flow chart creates a visual of the series of MMs referenced in Figure 15.2. You can start from anywhere on the flow chart. It will reinforce how a series of MMs progresses through a trend. It will also help a trader to know where they are in a particular trend. Most trends start with traditional MMs and can continue to trade in that cycle. It is important to reinforce what a trader's two triggers are:

1. A trade hits its profit target and does not stop. An extension begins.
2. A trade breaks its 61.8 percent level and fails its trend.

Everything that changes in the market revolves around these two events.

■ Why Is This Important to Your Trading?

Algorithms inside our modern markets don't predict price action. They exist in a cause and effect relationship with existing patterns in the market. Knowing that they don't know or care whether the market goes up or down is a liberating concept to most traders. Computer algorithms don't pick tops or bottoms in the market. They wait for trends to break, and ride the wave of price action until it fails.

The power and volume in the markets are created by these algorithms. It is said that 90 percent of the volume in the markets is traded by computers. Computer algorithms have rules preventing them from picking tops and bottoms. This simple fact should give us more reason not to fight the trend. As retail traders, we are the equivalent of ants in the Serengeti of Africa. It is impossible to move the market by ourselves. Our job as traders is to grab hold of the coattails of the *smart money* and hitch a ride to our profit targets.

For more information, watch the video titled "Using the Past to Predict the Future," available at http://eminiaddict.com/?p=5617.

The Trading Plan

Keeping Yourself Safe with Statistical-Based Rules

There are as many different ways to trade the markets as there are people who trade them. No trading strategy will be successful without four elements.

■ The Four Legs of a Trading Strategy

It's easy to think about these elements in relation to a chair with four legs. A chair needs all four legs to be functional and stand on its own. The same is true for a trading strategy. Without these four elements or legs, any trading strategy will fail. Some trading strategies have very specific rules for entry and no rules for taking profit. Other trading strategies might have very specific rules for profit taking, but have no specific rules to protect profits once they are acquired. Even trading strategies that follow strict money management principles will fail if they do not have specific entry and exit points. What most trading strategies focus on is how to enter into the market. That is the easy part. The ultimate goal of the trading plan is to design statistical-based rules. Statistical-based rules allow you to enter, exit, and hold on to profit. Ninety percent of all volume in our modern markets is traded by computers. The rise of computer algorithms has made statistical-based rules even more profitable. As traders, our job is to grab onto the coattails of those trading algorithms. By grabbing on, you're able to trade on the path of least resistance and take advantage of the algorithm's volume. Traders face an incredible challenge when beginning their careers. The goal is to give you these trading rules so that you do not have to make the same mistakes. Trading rules come from learning from one's mistakes. In adopting these concepts and rules, you are putting yourself on a fast track to trading success. There are two types of people in this world. The first type is quite common; they are forced to learn their own mistakes. The second type of person is the one that learns from others' mistakes. These people are the true geniuses of the world and are quite rare. Sir Isaac Newton once said, "If I've accomplished anything, it is because I stood on the shoulders of giants."

Leg 1: Money Management

Money management is where most traders fail. Most traders start their career thinking, "I'll just give it a try." Usually, what they end up doing is starting overleveraged with a gambler's mentality. Risking 1 percent or less per trade is a rule that must never be broken. It is the difference between being the casino and being the gambler. We all know how that works out in Vegas. The casino always wins the profits from the gamblers. It is also true in the market. Adopt the casino's mentality and think of your trading career as a marathon instead of a sprint. Statistical-based rules allow you to profit over time. If you're trading correctly, it will actually turn into a job. The reason this book was written, and the reason you are reading it, is to understand your new job requirements. The 1 percent rule will help you keep your emotions in check. Risking 1 percent will help you in making good decisions, especially in times of uncertainty. Position-sizing calculators are available, and they're something that should be used every single day before the opening bell rings. Knowing your 1 percent risk keeps you from breaking the first cardinal rule of trading. Always associate risking the correct amount of capital with being profitable.

Leg 2: Entry Rules

Entry rules are very specific. We know based on our entry rules the specific prices to enter the market. Having specific entry strategies allows us to be consistent over time. Some traders like to wait and find out if a measured move (MM) or trade setup is going to work or not. What these traders don't understand is that if they don't take the trade setup with confidence, they end up chasing the market. Chasing markets will almost never work out profitably for a trader. It is easier to think of entering a trade this way. Enter an MM with confidence and conviction by following your entry rules, and it will be profitable. Waiting for a valid trade setup to see if it works will result in missing the trade. If the trader misses a trade setup, he or she is forced to chase the market. The question that must be asked is why did the trader fail to follow his or her entry rules? Failure to follow the entry rule is usually caused by fear. The fear is caused by overleverage and incorrect position sizing and money management rules. A trader who is following his money management rules has absolutely no reason not to take the trade setups that meet his criteria with confidence and conviction. Experienced traders immediately reduce the size of their trade if they feel uncertain about the trade setup. This is all in our heads. Instead of being scared of every single opportunity that the market makes available, shift into being scared to *not* take the trade setups that the market makes available. Go from being afraid to fulfill your job requirements to being profitable. William Bull Halsey, a four-star admiral in World War II, is credited with saying: *"All problems become smaller if you don't dodge them, but confront them. Touch a thistle timidly, and it pricks you; grasp it boldly, and its spines crumble."*

Leg 3: Profit-Taking Rules

Taking profit is a planned event. If you fail to follow your profit-taking rules, it becomes a reactionary event. The rule for profit taking is to always take profits at a profit target. If the trader has the ability to trade multiple contracts and can take partial profit, he must take profit. If a trader is trading only a single contract, he must end his trade and take profits. Each and every MM has its own unique entry and profit-taking spots. A profit target is where you get paid for following your money management and entry strategies. Taking profits at profit targets seems like an easy thing to do. Profit targets have their own unique challenges. When a trade is at its profit target, you are dealing with the exact opposite emotions you're dealing with at its entry. At an MM entry there is a fear of loss, or fear of not knowing whether the trade will work out. At a profit target there are feelings of euphoria and confidence. The emotions and thoughts that are running through a trader's head at a profit target are "I'm the best" and "I can squeeze way more profit out of this trade." The reality is that being greedy rarely results in more profits. If a trader does decide to stay in a trade past a profit target, he is knowingly risking all of his unrealized gains to see a continuation of a trend. If the trade setup is at the beginning of a much larger trend, then a trader could use a larger target. What usually happens in a situation like this is that a trader misses his profit-taking opportunity. After missing the profit-taking opportunity, the market will come all the way back down into its original entry location. That profit-taking opportunity ends up being a breakeven trade. The lesson here is to take what the market makes available to you and nothing more. There will always be another MM with its own unique profit target.

Leg 4: Statistical-Based Trading Rules

The fourth leg creates our solid foundation and encapsulates our entry, exit, and money management rules. Trading rules are developed by learning from one's mistakes. The only way that one learns from one's mistakes is to keep a trading journal. The only way to know if you've learned from a mistake is never making that same mistake again. Trading journals have evolved over the years. Years ago, retail traders had to record each and every trade by hand. Traders would have to record entries, exits, and outcomes at the end of the trading day. A successful journal also requires you to make notes about trades and the thoughts that you had at the time that you entered a trade. It is extremely hard to manually record all of this data after a long trading day. Modern technology allows us to bulk import our data into Internet-based or software-based trading journals. Once these trading journals are compiled with enough information, they are extremely valuable at analyzing where we are the most profitable as traders. An example of information we get out of trading journals is the best and worst times of the day trade. There are days of the week and weeks of the month that should be traded with lower risk. Trading rules help us understand where we are losing money. Once traders understand where they are losing money consistently, they can design trading rules to keep those losses from happening.

■ Why Trading Rules

A lesson learned from keeping a trading journal is having no trading zones. Some trading journals allow you to break down information into the most profitable minutes and hours of the day. Some trading journals will also let you sort through those trades that were profitable and find out where they originate. One of the most valuable pieces of information we have gathered over the years is the no-trade zone, between 9:30 and 10 A.M. Eastern Time.

Analyzing trading journals over time has shown us that losses are associated with that first half-hour of the trading day. Entries in the journal over time will tell us that trades that originate out of the 8 to 9:30 A.M. ET time frame are consistently profitable. Trades that originate between 9:30 and 10 A.M. ET have a very low expectation for positive results. A trader must learn to change his actions and avoid those losses. By avoiding this time frame, a trader can give himself a raise. Sometimes in trading it's not how much you make that matters, but how much you keep.

Keeping a trading journal will tell you over time that entering between 10 and 10:15 A.M. ET produces favorable and profitable trades. Traders will notice over time that 10 A.M. is where a rush of volume comes into the market. These pieces of data will help you develop rules to trade more efficiently and more profitably.

Trading rules are divided into four different categories:

1. General Trading Account Rules
2. Gap Fill Rules
3. American (NYSE) Trading Rules
4. European (Euro) Trading Rules

■ General Trading Account Rules

Never add money to the account. Some traders like to "try out" futures trading. They start with small accounts, and then over leverage those small accounts. Starting with the correct size account and using the correct risk percentage at the very beginning is the best policy. Having to add money to an account to continue trading also signals a problem that needs to be solved.

Never place a trade without a stop loss. Placing stop losses on trades should be automatic. With modern advanced trade management systems, stops can be specified before the trade is even filled. There is no reason a trader should not use a stop loss. Traders who don't use stops will find that it will only be a matter of time before this bad habit hurts them.

Have a target for every trade. Every trade is planned before it is entered. Without a target there is no trade. If a trade does not have a target, there is no way to know what the risk-reward ratio is. If a trader does not know the risk-reward ratio, he has no business entering a trade.

Enter trades at MMs in the direction of the trend. You often hear traders say "go with the flow" or "trade the trend." Do not fight the major trend in the market. Let the larger time frames show you the path of least resistance.

Use limit orders. Be specific about the price you want. Every trade is planned before it is entered. Without a specific entry there is no trade. If a trader does not have a specific entry, he does not know where his stop will be. If a trader does not know the risk-reward ratio, he has no business entering a trade.

Never risk more than 1 percent of total trading capital per trade. The most important rule in trading is to not overleverage your account. All of the problems that traders face stem from fears and emotions. By risking the correct percentage of capital per trade, 90 percent of those problems traders face disappear.

Do NOT try to "sell highs" and "buy lows" just because the price is trading at a major support or resistance level. Wait for the technical failure in the most recent series of MMs. Avoid the tendency to try to pick tops or bottoms. The best and safest thing to do is to wait for a trend break at a major support or resistance level. By waiting for the trend to break you are following the same rules that the algorithms follow. The market's trend will tell us everything we need to know about the direction of the market.

Do NOT rush a trade unless parameters are defined before the trade is placed. There will always be another opportunity; there is no reason to chase the market. A trade that was not planned should not be traded. If you see the trade and you are not a part of it, it is over. Wait for the next MM to develop.

Focus on trading effectively and follow your rules. Traders get caught up in focusing on the money. This causes their emotions to rule their decision-making process. Instead, try to focus on following your trading rules to the best of your ability. Try to associate following your rules with profit and breaking your rules with losses. A trader who follows his or her trading rules best wins in the end.

Trade half position size on Mondays, Fridays, options expiration, Rollover Thursdays, and Fridays after the futures rollover.

The financial markets' workweek is like any other line of work. Friday's productivity ends after lunch on Friday afternoon. All anyone can think about is what they're going to do over the weekend. The same is true of any Monday morning in any line of work. On Mondays everyone is dragging their feet into work. Productivity picks up after lunch on Monday afternoon and continues with its normal volume and participation throughout the week, until Friday afternoon. Trade these days of the week with lower risk. It is important to lower your risk on Mondays and Fridays, and if you cannot lower your risk or trade a smaller-sized contract, you should consider not trading at all. Friday afternoons and Monday mornings consistently provide choppy, range-bound markets. Tuesdays through Thursdays are trending, high-participation markets. Option expiration Fridays and futures rollover are also considered reduced-sized days.

■ Gap Fill Trading Rules

The best time to enter a gap fill trade is between 8 and 8:30 A.M. EST.

E-mini S&P 500 Index (ES) gaps should be as least 5 points and not more than 10 points. If it doesn't meet the criteria, pass on the trade. Passing on gap fills that are less than five points is merely a case of the reward not being worth the risk.

If it's a professional gap and doesn't fill, then look for the first buy/sell signal in the direction of the gap. When the market opens up 10 points above or below the previous day's closing price you have a professional gap. A trader is required to trade the trend away from the gap fill and trail it until it fails. Once the trend moving away from the gap fill fails, a trader then has an opportunity to trade the next MM in the direction of the gap fill.

Record unfilled gaps and keep their price level handy; the market will often fill open gaps later on in the week. Your record of unfilled gaps will become valuable information weeks and months later.

Stay in the trade until the gap fills or the stop is hit. The market may attempt to retest its original entry. In this situation, it is better not to micromanage a gap fill trade. A retest will normally not stop out an original entry; it will merely touch it again. A trader maximizes his initial risk-reward ratio by staying in the gap fill trade until the target is hit or the trade is stopped out.

Avoid gap plays on options expiration Fridays, rollover Thursdays, and the first trading day of the new month. It's okay to play gap-up situations, as the markets have a tendency to run away and produce professional gap-and-goes.

After a narrow-range day, if the next day's gap is larger than the previous day's range, or the market's opening prices are outside the previous day's session high or low, stay away from a gap fill.

Imagine the market being in a tight consolidation for a day and then overnight it breaks out or breaks down. The consolidation has produced fuel for the gap, and it will always be dangerous to try to fight the gap fill on days like this.

The one key point to remember is that the ES is the leader in the most technical market for the gap fill. The other indices such as the E-mini Dow Jones Index (YM), E-mini Russell 2000 Index (TF), and E-mini Nasdaq 100 Index (NQ) also have gap fills that can be traded. One can use the ES futures as a leading indicator to trade the other indices into their own gap fills. The easiest way to take profit at the gap fill in these other indices is to take profit on them when the ES completes its gap fill. The reason for this is that when the ES completes its gap fill, the algorithms also take profit on the other indices. Sometimes this can keep the other indices from filling their gaps completely.

■ American (NYSE) Session Trading Rules

Trading plans are never truly finished; they evolve over time. Trade setup guidelines are as follows:

It is extremely important to only take the 50 percent setups that occur in 15-minute charts. Trading only the 15-minute MMs helps us filter our trades. Trading too small a time frame can lead to overtrading. Where there might only be five to seven MMs that exist during a trading day, there are many more on the smaller time frames. The MMs on the 15-minute charts also have better risk-reward ratios. When you are making a decision on whether to place a trade, make sure that you are trading the path of least resistance in the direction of the larger time frames.

Another way to help us filter our trades is to monitor market breadth. If market breadth is strong and increasing, look for only MM longs to trade. This helps us choose the trades we take more efficiently. Just the opposite is true in weak markets.

If market breadth is weak and decreasing, look for only MM shorts to trade. Trade the path of least resistance.

The NYSE Tick chart helps us time our entries. When we are in a series of MM longs, we look for low ticks to buy in anticipation of the continuation of the long trend. Just the opposite is true when the market is trading a series of MM shorts. We look for high ticks to sell in anticipation of the continuation of the short trend.

If, for whatever reason, a trade fails to get initiated at the first test of an MM, check "time and sales" to confirm participation in the second test. The second test is considered the most dangerous test, as all of the initial participants' positions will be under pressure. There needs to be a whole new group of participants to offset the potential shakeout of the initial MM.

Another way to help traders filter the MMs they trade requires the Nasdaq Bank to confirm the move in the direction of the trade.

Each trading day can be broken down into two trading sessions. The first trading session is from 8 to 11:30 A.M. ET. The second trading session is from 1:30 to 4 P.M. ET. The only exception is the no-trade zone between 9:30 and 10 A.M. ET. All trades must be initiated *only* during these two time frames. The only exception is for the management of existing trades that are still on. The biggest reason to stick to these two trade sessions is to stay out of the market during the times of the day that are the slowest. Many newer traders think that slower markets equal safety. The reality is that the low-volume and slow times of the day are the most dangerous. With little to no volume or participation, the markets will frustrate traders putting on new positions.

It is very important to not initiate any new trades after 3:45 P.M. The last 15 minutes of the day are some of the most volatile of the day. This no-trade zone is very similar to the no-trade zone at the beginning of the day. Institutional traders are interested in hedging their positions at the end of the day. Often, this hedging is done with market orders. When there are market orders and reactionary traders putting on and pulling off positions with market orders, price action can be fast and dangerous.

At the end of each day, it is important to review the day and the opportunities that the market made available. Applying your trading rules to the market after it closes increases emotional capital. At the end of the day, if you have followed your trading rules, you should congratulate yourself. Associate following your trading rules with being profitable, and breaking them with incurring losses.

■ European (Euro) Session Trading Rules

The goal of any trade plan is to grow accounts. Growing accounts comes from two different types of trades. The two different types of trade are the intraday income trade and the longer-term wealth creation trade. The intraday trade is just that, more than likely closed by the end of the day. The wealth creation trade is longer term in nature, lasting a week or longer. The currency markets, specifically the euro spot market and all the instruments associated with it, are easier to trade in longer-term wealth creation trades.

The main goal in trading the currencies, specifically the EUR/USD, is to identify the trend and trade on the path of least resistance. The larger the time frame, the more important and powerful the trend will be. When trading the currencies, a trade does not have the luxury of any of the intraday tools that exist during the NYSE trading session. This makes identifying the longer-term trend extremely important. Trade the path of least resistance and ignore or filter out all the opportunities that exist against the major trend.

The next goal is to categorize high-probability setups in terms of risk versus reward and place the highest priority on best trades. The lower the risk-reward ratio, the less priority it will have.

The contractor analogy is a great analogy to choosing the best trades to take. If you owned a company and had only enough manpower for one job in a week, how would you choose which job to take if you had two options? Let's imagine that each job has the same profit at the completion of the work. One job is a 1-hour drive and the other is 15 minutes away. The job that is closest has the best risk-reward ratio due to the fact that there is less cost involved. The best risk-reward ratio will always win. As it is with trading, the better the risk-reward ratio, the more participants it will have. The more participants it has, the higher the likelihood of its reaching its target.

Times to trade the EUR/USD are from 3:00 to 11:30 A.M. ET. Times not to trade or to trade slower (i.e., managing positions and stops) are any time after the European close at 11:30 A.M. ET. After the European close, the euro will go almost completely silent. Just as the NYSE enters the daily doldrums, European markets are closing. Trading the euro after 11:30 A.M. ET will result in choppy and slow markets. Often, this slow time of the day will trade within a 10-pip range for the rest of the day until the Asian Session begins.

■ Setups

This section contains overview information on different kinds of setups.

Daily Setups

Our highest-priority MMs are the daily setups and usually happen once a week. Every week we should expect one to be completing its profit target (hitting a –23 percent target). These are your highest-reward trades and should be focused on throughout the week. We should always know where the next trade is in our trend. These trades can be identified 24 to 36 hours before they happen. Knowing where these larger MMs begin gives the trader an enormous window of opportunity to participate in the trend.

15-Minute Setups

Fifteen-minute setups should be taken with the trend on the daily charts. These are your second-highest-priority setups and are the basis for most of the intraday trades that are made available to us on a weekly basis. There can be anywhere from three to seven MMs that exist on the medium-term time frame during a single trading day.

Micro Setups

Micro setups should be taken in the direction of the daily and 15-minute setups. These are your least-priority trades, but can help you enter into a larger 15-minute or daily trend. Think of the micro trend as an entry tool into the larger risk versus reward trades. They can be used as income trades but, because of the possibility of overtrading, should be used with caution.

■ A Trading Journal

The most important trading rule is to use a trading journal. If you're trading without a journal, you have wasted all of the opportunities to learn from your mistakes. Each time you paid tuition to the market was an opportunity to learn something about your nature as a trader. In the past, the problem with trading journals was that you had to manually record all of your trades. After a long trading day, the motivation to update your journal would quickly disappear. Trading journals have come a long way. No longer do you have to manually record all of your trades, you can now bulk upload your trades into a journal. Modern trading journals can break your profitability down to even the minutes of the day. They can track your profitably per days of the week and months of the year. If we are not learning from our mistakes, then we are bound to repeat them.

The trading rules in this chapter are based on years of data recorded in trading journals. For example: the no-trade zone of the first half hour of the day; restricting yourself to 15-minute setups during the daily doldrums. These are examples of learning from one's mistakes. If you haven't used a training journal thus far, start today and never stop recording your data. Everyone is different, and everyone has different tendencies that can hurt them while trading. Your goal is to find out where you lose money. If you can identify where you're losing money consistently, you can add to these trading rules and make your cracks of weakness much narrower. Eventually, being a profitable trader is more about keeping the money you make. While the rules discussed are general trading rules to start with, each individual trader will have his or her own unique struggles to overcome, and may need to mold the rules to aid with particular weaknesses.

■ Why Is This Important to Your Trading?

It doesn't matter what kind of trader you are. The patterns in our markets produce long-term swing trades that can last a year or more. They can produce seasonal swing trades that last less than a year. They produce intraday swing trades that can last from days to weeks, or intraday setups that you can use to produce income. How you decide what kind of trader you are depends on the amount of time that you can reserve for the markets. When you're trying to decide whether you are an intraday or swing trader, analyze what times that you have available for the markets. The more time you have, the more you can choose to trade income and swing trades. If you have less time, seasonal swing trades might be your best option. Every trader is on a unique journey of self-discovery. I hope this information serves as a good base for your future development.

■ Bringing It all Together

My motivation for writing this book came from long hours of trial and error aspiring to be a successful trader. Countless hours of back testing indicators, and the triumph of seeing stacks of books that I had read led me to want to share what I had learned.

After I had read everything that I could about trading, I had to throw out what didn't work. All of the information floating around in my head needed to be consolidated and simmered down to what was most important in being profitable: specific entries, stops, and profit targets. It was only after I removed all of the indicators and *forgot* everything that I had learned that I was able to see these patterns in the market. My hope is that after the trial and error, the practice and preparation, and the time it took me to recognize these patterns, they will come to you in a fast and efficient form. You do not have to go through the same trials; you can sidestep the mistakes and form a solid foundation of trading proficiently. When I discovered these patterns in the market it literally changed my life. I want to share these patterns and trading techniques with as many people as I can.

You are now in the group of people that are considered "in the know." You know how the markets work and how price moves for from one pattern to another. If you're reading this, you started out much like I did. You're not a born trader, but no one is. The majority of people reading this book did not start out as traders. You're starting from somewhere in the middle of nowhere, aspiring to make yourself and your life situation better. Many times, doctors' children end up being doctors themselves. Lawyers' children end up becoming lawyers. I would bet that you did not come from a trading family or grow up "in the know." I applaud you for your tenacity and drive for making it this far. I hope that the knowledge that I leave you with affects your life positively and profitably. In disciplined and patient hands, this knowledge can change future generations in astounding ways. It all begins with you. I would like to personally thank you for taking the time to read this book. I feel extremely fortunate and blessed to be able to share this knowledge. May your future be bright and full of profit targets.

ABOUT THE AUTHOR

David Halsey is founder of the website EminiAddict.com, a site that provides trader education and market commentary. His focus is day trading and swing trading stock index futures utilizing techniques designed to stay on the right side of institutional order flow and identify short-term setups. He provides a daily market analysis, predictions, and an interactive forum for his subscribers. His videos are utilized by several brokerage firms and disseminated to their clients.

INDEX

Printed and bound by CPI Group (UK) Ltd, Croydon, CR0 4YY

16/04/2025

14658451-0003